Older Workforces

We are all going to become old. Many countries are ageing demographically with ageing workforces. Despite anti-discrimination and equality laws, older workers are routinely left out from learning opportunities even unconsciously so, suffer stereotyping or they simply do not participate. Why is this so? This book looks to understand the background to this and re-imagine older workplaces to capitalise on older workers.

The author explores what learning and development offers a best fit for older workforces through literature, research and case studies with organisations and individuals. She considers how an organisation might shift its strategic processes to offer a holistic workforce opportunity of value to both employee and employer, as it is cognitive skills that will be needed in future workforces.

Emphasising the area of work agency and the human right to learning, this book turns ageing and learning in workplaces on its head, seeing older workers as vessels of untapped potential. It re-imagines their possibilities in a time of intense demographic and digital change. This book will be a pragmatic guide to academics, researchers and practitioners in the fields of workplace learning, human resource development, social policy and diversity.

Domini Bingham is Lecturer in Educational Leadership at the Institute of Education, UCL, United Kingdom. She leads on several modules of the MBA (Educational Leadership), MA Leadership and MA AELM (Masters in Applied Educational Leadership and Management). She researches in the areas of ageing, older workplaces, leading for wellbeing, workplace learning and citizenship in schools. She is a former adult teacher with a wider professional background in international development, the media and marketing. She has previously worked at the Commonwealth Secretariat and as Deputy Literary Editor of *The Mail on Sunday*, in the film industry and in public relations. She is a Chartered Marketer and Fellow of the Chartered Institute of Marketing and a Teaching Fellow, Advance HE.

Older Workforces

Re-imagining Later Life Learning

Domini Bingham

Routledge
Taylor & Francis Group
LONDON AND NEW YORK

First published 2019
by Routledge

2 Park Square, Milton Park, Abingdon, Oxfordshire OX14 4RN
52 Vanderbilt Avenue, New York, NY 10017

Routledge is an imprint of the Taylor & Francis Group, an informa business

First issued in paperback 2020

British Library Cataloguing-in-Publication Data
A catalogue record for this book is available from the British Library

Library of Congress Cataloging-in-Publication Data
Names: Bingham, Domini, author.
Title: Older workforces : re-imagining later life learning / Domini Bingham.
Description: 1 Edition. | New York : Routledge, 2019. | Includes bibliographical references and index.
Identifiers: LCCN 2018051737| ISBN 9781472470539 (hardback) | ISBN 9781315598789 (ebook)
Subjects: LCSH: Older people--Employment. | Employees--Training of. | Organizational learning.
Classification: LCC HD6279 .B476 2019 | DDC 658.3/120846--dc23
LC record available at https://lccn.loc.gov/2018051737

ISBN: 978-1-4724-7053-9 (hbk)
ISBN: 978-0-367-66210-3 (pbk)

Typeset in Bembo
by Integra Software Services Pvt. Ltd.

This book is dedicated to my sister Pieta Blomfield, who died suddenly in 2017.

Work thus belongs to the vocation of every person; indeed, a human being expresses and fulfils himself by working. At the same time, work has a "social" dimension through its intimate relationship not only to the family, but also to the common good, since "it may be said that it is only by the labor of working men that states grow rich."

Centesimus Annus ("The Hundreth Year"), St John Paul II,
1991 #6. © Libreria Editrice Vaticana

Contents

Figures

Foreword

My interest in older workers' learning fuses three areas of interest and research; that of older workers and workplaces, adult learning and development and well-being in the workplace and the intersection between the three.

Having explored adult learning for a number of years and through my experience as a teacher of adults over a number of years, I have come to realise the complexity related to adult learning and engagement and participation in that learning and how lack of opportunities and barriers throw up major challenges in adults in realising their potential, such as time limitations due to work, family commitments, caring responsibilities and the necessity to earn money.

In exploring older workers' learning I have also deciphered that there are barriers which represent deep-rooted inequalities across societies and organisations through a study of one higher education site.

This book originally set out to be a work on older workers' learning taking the first two of my enduring interests but, as my understanding developed, the work has transformed into a close scrutiny of diversity and inclusion and older workers' learning as it became evident to me that it is not possible to critically interpret one area without a consideration of the other two. There is a close relationship and intersectionality between diversity, well-being and learning which this book has sought to explore. Thus, this book has coalesced into a triad of themes of flourishing and empowerment for older workers and their development needs for mutual benefit, through enabling workplace structures, when otherwise older workers might withdraw from the workplace.

Looking for a bridge between existing theories of development and aligning the theories of flourishing, agency and empowerment it proposes a new organisational structure addressing the needs of older workers arguing for different requirements across the life course. Drawing on work agency and organisational theories, the book conceptualises a reciprocal and interdependent model suggesting a paradigm shift in organisational human resource development. Some of the work aligns with Kandola and Fullerton's (2003) diversity framework including elements of a skilled workforce, aware and fair, mission, objective and fair processes, active flexibility, individual focus and a culture that empowers where the links between a diversity-oriented organisation and the learning organisation are made explicit. However, Kandola and Fullerton state:

> Managing diversity should not be seen as separate from the learning organisation; it should instead be striving to refresh such approaches with the principles of diversity by adopting a symbiotic approach
>
> (Kandola and Fullerton 2003:166)

This book endeavours to close that gap by expanding the connection between managing diversity and workplace learning. Its contribution to international research is through building on socio-contextual relationships and processes in approaches to workplace learning relative to the structure-agency debate. Relational factors of empowerment and flourishing for older workers addressing individual work agency can be enablers in workplace structures and climates for learning but are contextual.

This book seeks to extend understanding of how ageing impacts on workplace learning in an under-researched area through accentuating that linking theories of empowerment and flourishing for individual work agency are central to learning being activated for older workers. The connection underlines what organisational structures and processes best support older workers' learning in modern workplaces for mutual gain when rising to the growing organisational challenge of demographic change, extended employability and a digital workplace, leading to a re-imagining of learning possibilities.

To follow my development and thinking around older workers and to contribute your own thoughts follow me on Twitter @DominiBingham

Reference

Kandola, R., and Fullerton, J. (2003). *Diversity in Action: Managing the Mosaic.* London: CIPD.

Acknowledgements

The data underpinning this book were made possible by the conversations with participants in the higher education study and other organisation and individual interviews and by those that contributed case studies. I would like to thank everyone who gave freely of their time, and in many cases, gave me encouragement.

To my friends, family and work colleagues, especially Professor Karen Evans, Dr Natasha Kersh, Dr Max Coates and Elizabeth Wood who accompanied me through the highs and lows of the writing and researching journey. To my son Miles, who has given and continues to give his continued support in my lifelong learning.

I thank you all.

Abbreviations

BME	Black and Minority Ethnic
BAME	Black, Asian and Minority Ethnic
CEDEFOP	European Centre for the Development of Vocational Training
CIPD	Chartered Institute of Personnel and Development
CROW	Centre for Research into the Older Workforce
ESRC	Economic and Social Research Council
ISS	Ideal Speech Situations
HEFCE	Higher Education Funding Council for England
HEI	Higher Education Institution
HESA	Higher Education Statistics Agency
HRM	Human Resource Management – sometimes referred to simply as human resources (HR)
ILO	International Labour Organization
KPI	Key Performance Indicators
LGBT	Lesbian, gay, bisexual and transgender
NIACE	National Institute of Adult Continuing Education
OLDER WORKERS	For this study Older workers are defined as aged 50+
OECD	Organisation for Economic Co-operation and Development
ONS	Office for National Statistics (UK)
PIACC	Programme for the International Assessment of Adult Competencies (OECD)
SOAD	Staff Organisation and Development
TLRP	Teaching and Learning Research Programme (TLRP 2000-9), Economic and Social Research Council (ESRC)
UCU	University College Union

UNISON	Amalgamation of three public sector trade unions, the National and Local Government Officers Association (NALGO), the National Union of Public Employees (NUPE) and the Confederation of Health Service Employees (COHSE)
WEF	World Economic Forum

1 Introduction

The context of ageing populations

This book is set against the context of ageing populations where those of an older age make up an increasing share of the population and where extended working lives, that is older people staying on in the workplace, are here to stay. This phenomenon is seen in contemporary workplaces across many countries.

The phenomenon is set against a landscape of changing demographics whereby increasing numbers of older workers across most developed countries are needed to fill the workforce gap. Yet, employers, organisations, governments and policymakers have been tardy, even reluctant to address the challenge of making use of older people and the implications of keeping increasing numbers of older workers engaged in the workplace. The situation will become ever more pressing as the workforce gap will only be increasing as it is suggested that there is a potential worldwide gap of 38–40 million high-skilled workers, representing 13% of demand for such workers. Whereas, there will potentially be a surplus of 90–95 million low-skilled workers around the world representing 10% of demand (McKinsey 2012).

The OECD recognises that year on year there is an increasing requirement for digital skills where almost 40% of adults lack basic skills to solve problems in technology rich environments (OECD 2018a). A shortage of cognitive and social skills is rising (ibid.) and it is the lower skilled most at risk of automation of jobs who are receiving less training.

This book therefore sheds light on an increasingly contemporary concern of widespread application to policymakers. One approach to encouraging older worker retention would be through older workers being given and taking up learning and development opportunities. This approach raises several questions.

How might older workers remain engaged for learning through development and training in the workplace and when they will make up an ever-larger segment of the workforce in many, mainly developed countries? And where, due to the "pension gap" across many countries, some workers have little choice but to continue working anyway and may display some dissatisfaction or lack of motivation? To what extent do managers of organisations value training and development of older workers and their contribution to workplaces? Where might the gaps lie in understanding this phenomenon? This book also raises questions and proposes tentative responses to training and development related to changing demography, a research issue identified by the European Commission in its report (EU 2011) on adult education trends and approaches, raising the role of older workers in today's workplaces. The report stated:

> Suddenly older workers are being regarded as important prospective members of the labour force (Mayo 2011:xiv), more innovative work practices and learning measures for older workers are required, which can be supported by bringing forward their voice and utilising their initiative.
>
> (EAEA 2012:4)

Classifying older workers

A definition of an older worker is one aged 50+ years according to the Department for Work and Pensions (DWP 2017) in the UK. However, the age at which you become an "older worker" varies across countries. The European Union (EU) Lisbon framework relevant to all 26 countries of the EU, cites older workers as between 55–64 (Tikkanen and Nyhan 2006) but does not mention those aged 65+. Perhaps it is not so much terminology but rather a question of an organisation's practice and culture when labelling certain workers as older (ibid.).

In the UK, the Department for Work and Pensions classification of an older workers as aged 50+ years (DWP 2017) has a strong resonance in the UK where it marks the point at which there is a decline in labour market participation, reported age discrimination and growing awareness of approaching retirement (McNair 2011). Set against a steeply rising pension gap, and rising life expectancy, the classification already could need an upward reconfiguration. Furthermore, people of working age in the UK are defined by DWP (2017) as aged 16–64. This definition is rapidly becoming outdated as for the first time over 10% of the UK workforce, representing over one million people, is aged over 65 (DWP 2017).

In the UK, the government has dismissed the default retirement age (DRA), a legal ruling on workforces stipulating when an older worker can be asked to retire by its employees. Now, formally workers are free to retire when they want to. The UK government states that the retirement age since abolishing DRA, is now supposedly "when an employee chooses to retire" (Gov UK 2012). Most businesses do not set a compulsory retirement age for their employees and if an employee chooses to work longer they cannot be discriminated against (ibid.).

In other countries, governments have encompassed similar policies to better retain older workers. However, in practice, the freedom to choose when to retire or indeed to stay on at work in the case of older workers may be curtailed by being managed out or forced out of their posts. Alternatively, they may be subjected to other unwanted stresses such as a deficit organisational culture around older workers which has the effect of showing them the exit door. These areas raise serious legal issues of both discrimination and equality.

As relevant as considering the retention of older workers is whether they should be differentiated in terms of their learning and development, as a widely held view is that late career workers do not invest heavily in their careers (Greller 2006). However, to the contrary, evidence from a US study of 450 US college-educated men aged 23–70 found age was not a factor in the hours spent on professional development and business networking. Findings of career motivation, measured as hours invested, showed the association was as strong for those in later careers as for younger workers, implying factors influencing investment in the former are similar (ibid.).

Increasing the employability and retention of older workers

In considering how to respond to the changing nature and size of ageing workforces across countries, policy responses are required to address three interrelated areas of concern: participation of older people in the workforce linked to withdrawal from the job market, policies to increase employment and retention and underemployment of older workers.

Across the EU, labour participation rates are causing concern particularly related to those aged 60+. While approximately 60% of Europeans aged 55–59 are employed this percentage is halved for those aged 60–64 in one third of member states, where no more than one in five workers in this age group is employed (EU 2011). In comparison, the rise in inactive people compared to those working is projected to increase to 70% of the populations of OECD countries by 2050 if there is no change in work and retirement patterns. This would reduce GDP per capita in OECD countries to 1.7% per annum over the next thirty years, a reduction of 30% from 1970–2000 (OECD 2006).

A link is made between adult education and the UN Sustainable Development Goals (SDGs) published in 2015, in particular SDG 4 (Ensure inclusive and equitable quality education and promote lifelong learning opportunities for all) (UN 2015). The 2015 UNESCO report emphasises the importance of lifelong learning as central to achieving full employment and supporting equity and inclusion for all and offers the opportunities for the realisation of other desirable objectives.

> We reaffirm that education is a public good, a fundamental human right and a basis for guaranteeing the realisation of other rights. It is essential for peace, tolerance, human fulfilment and sustainable development. We recognise education as key to achieving full employment and poverty

> eradication. We will focus our efforts on access, equity and inclusion, quality and learning outcomes, within a lifelong learning approach.
>
> (UNESCO et al. 2015:iii)

The "Live Longer, Work Longer" report (OECD 2006) of 21 member countries emphasised growing numbers of elderly people across many countries, partly as a consequence of the ageing of the 1960s "baby boomers" and also increased life expectancy. The report argues for an overhaul of employment and social policies, practices and attitudes to encourage work at an older age. This is at a time when there has been a significant decline in the prime working age population, defined as between ages 25 and 54, and evidenced from an analysis of 20 labour market indicators of over 200 countries (ILO 2003). A country's national policy and government regulation context, relative to age, strongly affects the participation of older workers in the labour market and their retirement decisions. Attitudes and policies of particular importance are related to pensions, employment protection legislation, wage policies and occupational and wider healthcare provision. Raising the statutory age at which workers can retire has become an important measure for increasing participation among older workers in the labour market (EU 2011). Other factors are also emphasised as being of significance.

> Several factors accounted for reduction in and withdrawal from the labour market including skills obsolescence and choosing not to take up roles at variance with personal value systems, e.g. looking for a better work–life balance to concentrate on health or family. However, research considered that discriminatory attitudes and beliefs are the main barriers to the labour force retention of older workers.
>
> (EU 2011:17)

Since the OECD report "Live Longer, Work Longer" (OECD 2006), attempts have been made to address the demographic challenge to workplaces, seen across many countries. The abovementioned 2012 EU report on 34 countries, indicated (where data available) a variety of impacts including an increase in employment of older workers, in exit ages from the labour market and in numbers of workers choosing to work past retirement age. One way to offset the negative decline in growth is to improve job prospects (others are increasing immigration, improving productivity or achieving higher levels of fertility) by either helping older workers stay in work longer, thereby slowing the levels of inactive people, or encouraging them back into the workplace. The same 2012 EU report highlighted several areas where the UK needed to improve its employment rate for older people.

However, the implementation of any policy for continued participation in work by older workers is complicated. For example, Australian research points to a broad generalisation and paradox for managers in that the Australian government, in favour of retaining an older workforce, has urged employers to retain older workers. But in this study many employers either eschewed older workers or were not inclined to explore alternative conditions under which their employment might be of benefit. Similarly, many older workers in the same research indicated they would prefer to retire and seemed equally unwilling to explore alternative conditions where they could continue to work, perhaps in a reduced capacity (Patrickson and Ranzijn 2005).

As referred to above, a UK policy response to increasing employment, and to tackle employment barriers on the side of employers, has been to abolish the DRA. In many countries, pension reform policies to change the way people save through occupational pensions have been made to encourage saving for retirement (OECD 2015b). However, financial insecurities, coupled with a "pension gap," means those wishing to retire cannot, so increasingly older workers are obliged to stay on in the workplace, regardless of a desire to retire, through an extended working life, or voluntarily staying on as life expectancy increases.

Underemployment is a further concern. A definition of underemployment refers to workers who accept jobs that do not fully utilise their skills (McNair 2011) and a growing proportion of workers aged 50–70 report being very overqualified for their jobs which represents a significant waste of talent even though some workers choose to move to less stressful roles (ibid.). Being underemployed in this context raises the issue as to the extent to which an older worker can flourish in the workplace and can stimulate an early exit from the workforce.

Participation and retention of older people in employment is also influenced by provision for education and training across workplaces (EU 2011). Encouraging increased levels of participation the "Agenda for New Skills and Jobs" Initiative (EU 2011:9), to prolong the working lives of older people, called for "a more targeted approach to lifelong learning and career guidance" to ensure more vulnerable groups, including older workers benefit. Guidelines include approaches for improving participation in labour markets, encouraging active ageing to reduce structural unemployment and promoting job quality.

Two guidelines are particularly relevant (EU 2011):

> Work–life balance policies with the provision of affordable care and innovation in the manner in which work is organised should be geared to raising employment rates, particularly among [. . .] older workers.
>
> (Guideline 7)

> To develop a skilled workforce responding to labour market needs and promoting lifelong learning efforts should focus on [. . .] increasing the employability of older workers.
>
> (Guideline 8)

Responding to the workforce demographic challenge

In terms of how far the recommendations of the "Live Longer, Work Longer" report (OECD 2006) have been implemented, a follow-up assessment made by the OECD (2015a) of improvement made between 2004–2012, although indicating that some progress had been made across countries, also suggested that more needs to be done. On the positive side, for example, the same 2006 OECD report identifies that labour market prospects for older workers in the UK between 2006–2012 had improved. In 2011, the employment rate for the population aged 50–64, in the United Kingdom, was 0.5 percentage points higher than in 2005 and 3.7 percentage points above the OECD average (ibid.). Between April and June 2012, 29 million people aged 18 and over were in work representing 59% of the UK population, 29% of the working population, representing 8.4 million workers, were aged 50+ (Gov UK 2012).

Action has been taken in the UK to improve employability through improved coordination in skill delivery and strengthening of career guidance provision to all, to include older adults, through the development of a joint strategic position to create the Education and Skills Funding Agency from 2017 as a single funding agency, sitting within the Department for Education (DfE 2017) which funds education and skills for children, young people and adults. Self-employment among older people, as a viable alternative to continuing to work for others is also being promoted, as are apprenticeships for older workers. Nevertheless, in 2018, an OECD report stated that there needs a greater policy effort and intervention in the UK to ensure that all workers are provided with opportunities to develop, maintain and upgrade their skills, thereby reducing the risk of becoming trapped in low-wage, low-quality jobs and joblessness (OECD 2018a). Equal opportunities policies have become more widespread, but practices have not (DWP 2017). The UK government have announced a new national retraining scheme to test innovative approaches to helping adults upskill and reskill which will coordinate lifelong learning. To be firstly run as a pilot, it will help to understand more about how to support and incentivise adults to learn skills that will help them, their local economies and national productivity (BEIS 2017).

Other countries have adopted a variety of initiatives to target older workers to a greater or lesser success. However, the OECD (2015b) review notes that policies across the OECD countries to continue to promote age diversity in employment were moving ahead with implementing anti-age discrimination legislation. In the case of the UK, promotion of a more welcoming and more flexible working environment has continued. Also, some action has been taken to strengthen financial incentives to carry on working. Notwithstanding, in view of the faster rise of the state pension age for women from 60 to 65, an OECD (2006) recommendation to develop programmes to support women remaining in employment through early intervention and prevention for the age group 50–60 age group, to ensure that intervention did not come too late, was not acted upon.

Sociological and philosophical theoretical concepts around flourishing in the workplace

The central proposition presented in this book is that the achievement of flourishing and potential cannot and should not be the singular premise of younger workers. Older workers too, have a rightful claim to learning as "vessels of untapped potential." How older workers confronting extended working lives might be drawn into the "lifeworld" of the workplace and how restrictions associated with modernity and alienation could be challenged, are legitimate areas to explore. How older workers might achieve flourishing through engaging in dialogue, to realise their professional development have been investigated, alongside what organisational enabling structures and processes need to be present. Giving spaces for such dialogue permits the exploration of dilemmas and possibilities in how older workers approach professional practice. Management responses in exploring the views and understandings of older workers are also emphasised through examples, case studies and vignettes. This includes exploring what diversity and inclusion means to organisations in terms of professional development for older workers and how it is demonstrated, informally and formally, leading to a re-imagining of their learning possibilities and putting into place a re-envisioning of older workplaces. As the UNESCO Rethinking Education report (2015b) states:

> Learning is also crucial for empowerment and the development of capabilities to effect social transformation. Indeed, education can contribute to the more challenging task of transforming our mindset and our worldview
>
> (2015b:32)

To understand more deeply theories related to learning and the workplace for older workers, psychological, socio-cultural and postmodern theories are important as it is this intersection of factors which are most relevant to contemporary workplace learning (Evans et al. 2002; Unwin 2009; Hager 2010). Across this interdisciplinary scholarship, four overarching and interconnected theoretical fields inform an understanding of the empirical field:

- empowerment of older workers in having their voice heard in the workplace;
- flourishing of older workers, professional development through workplace learning in extending individual working lives;
- socio-contextual relationships and processes;
- enabling organisational structures, processes and relationships.

These four concepts which are each interconnected to notions of flourishing are further discussed in Chapter 3.

Figure 1.1 presents an initial conceptual framework drawing on the interdisciplinary nature of the literature. The conceptual framework themes emerge from the four concepts set out above. A philosophical assumption of an advocacy, participatory or emancipatory worldview held by theorists including Habermas (1987) and Freire (2005) consider "post-positivist assumptions imposed structural laws or theories not fitting marginalised individuals in society, or issues of social justice that needed to be addressed" and where

Fig 1.1 Older workers: conceptions of value in development in the workplace for mutual benefit

specific issues addressing empowerment, inequality and suppression may need action to address such concerns (Creswell 2009:9) aligns with the criticality for older workers to have opportunities for development. Sen's (1993) capability vectors or functionings which make up a broad framework for evaluating individual and social well-being also needs to be in place through enabling workplace structures to address concerns. It can be seen as providing a broad human development paradigm (Fukuda-Parr and Shiva Kumar 2003). However, Sen does not endorse a specific list or a well defined approach as each specification might consist of a different bundle of valued functionings. He views selection as based on reason; each approach will require its own list but must be context dependent, but Sen does stress the role of agency.

The human resource element, as the outside rim of the circle, provides the background to the entire concept as a strategic framework within which other elements are nested (Boxall and Purcell 2011). This outside rim represents the organisation while the components, shown in the inner circle, contribute to the flourishing of older workers as agentic individuals. The conceptual framework is informed by an interest in older workers' ability to flourish and be empowered in the workplace through learning. It represents the twin foundations of empowerment and flourishing for older workers' learning informed by the four elements discussed above.

The organisational structure recognises that a critical HR development strategy and processes provide an overarching umbrella for learning possibilities for older workers. Within this strategy, initiatives for learning arise from older workers' participation, alongside formal structures. Through enabling structures and processes, empowerment and flourishing through training and development can occur. There is an explicit two-way interaction, with the core facet being the notion of exercising capability and work agency through development. How older workers interact within the specific context is key. The approach is through dialogue and interaction to reach negotiated understanding and benefit, through creating dialogic spaces between staff and the overarching management structure in an organisational environment. A dialogic process connects each element, each enacting on the other in a cyclical and continuous process. This worldview aligned with it being critical for older workers to have opportunities for development and Sen's capability vectors in place through enabling workplace structures to address concerns.

The inclusion in this book of case studies and vignettes across different sectors and organisations around diversity management inform understandings of diversity and inclusion to establish an enabling workplace culture for older workers. Case studies also explore examples of good practice in learning and development for the older workforce enacted by organisations. As this book seeks to represent wider holistic notions of development for older workers, vignettes of development practice are included as well as case studies on health implications related to the improvement of well-being and healthy workplaces for older workers.

The empirical research forming the backbone of this book concerns the findings of twenty interviews and a survey conducted in one sector, that of higher education, focused on one English university. The findings are explored further in Chapter 3. However, the findings of this sector can be extended and applied to other sectors as the book sets out.

Making the business case for older workers in an ageing future

Currently, there is a limited blueprint of what an ageing future should look like, and where ageing is predominantly seen as a loss or decline rather than as an opportunity (Moody and Sasser 2012) although this is rapidly changing. For example, in work being undertaken by the World Health Organisation (WHO 2007) on age friendly cities, countries are adapting their environments to be more inclusive to the needs of growing numbers of senior citizens.

Related to working environments, both internal and external challenges are present across many organisations to implement policies and procedures around diversity and inclusion and the negative economic climate seen across many countries, following on from the financial crash of 2007, has stalled the efforts of organisations in their recruitment to increase diversity and inclusion. Nevertheless, there is growing awareness among policymakers and organisations across sectors that there is a valid business case for utilising older workers. A study by McKinsey (2015) "Diversity Matters," although not specifically citing age, reveals that companies ranked in the top 25% by diversity of their boards are 53% more profitable than those in the bottom 25%. A follow-up McKinsey report in 2018 (Hunt et al. 2018), indicates that the business case for diversity continues to be compelling. Companies in the top-quartile for ethnic/cultural diversity on executive teams were 33% more likely to have industry-leading profitability. That this relationship continues to be strong, suggests they say, that inclusion of highly diverse individuals – and the myriad ways in which diversity exists beyond gender (e.g., LGBTQ+, age/generation, international experience) – can be a key differentiator among companies.

Globalisation has resulted in sophisticated, fast-moving and competitive environments. To maintain success and sustainability, organisations must continually innovate and create new products and services. A diverse workforce is required to lead innovation and foster creativity. A multiplicity of voices across multigenerational workforces leads to new ideas, creativity and stimulates different ways of working. Many organisations no longer view having an emphasis on diversity and inclusion as being separate from their other business practices and recognise that a diverse workforce can differentiate them from their competitors through attracting top talent and capturing new clients (Forbes Insight Report 2011).

However, the triple challenge of ageing workforces, a declining pipeline of talent, and a requirement to manage multigenerational workforces are areas becoming critical for organisations to address to maintain a competitive edge (ibid.). The challenge in making a shift to digitalisation and increased automation is also rapidly becoming a huge challenge.

The golden age index

The Golden Age index compiled by PwC measures the extent to which different economies are harnessing the power of their older workers and captures a broad range of indicators relating to the participation of older people in employment and training. First published in 2015, it estimates how much each OECD economy could gain from raising employment rates for those aged over 55 to the levels of Sweden, the top performing EU country (Iceland and New Zealand being small island economies that seem less relevant as benchmarks for larger OECD economies like the US or the UK). The findings reveal that the OECD could add around $2.6 trillion to the total GDP in the long run if countries with a lower full-time equivalent employment rate among their older workers increased their rates to Swedish levels (PwC 2016).

The top three performing countries – Iceland, New Zealand and Sweden all have in common a focus on facilitating later and flexible retirement. Other high-ranking countries such as the US, Norway and

Korea have adopted a holistic approach to public policy and introduced anti-discrimination legislation. Meanwhile labour market policy for older workers in Japan, Germany and the UK aim to promote flexibility around the legal retirement age. Significantly, the analysis also suggests that policies to support older workers should not crowd out younger workers.

Three priorities emerge from the index.

- Firstly, governments should introduce policy measures to encourage or facilitate later retirement or flexible retirement (for example, Germany). This could be achieved through pension reform or by creating other financial incentives that encourage workers to continue working beyond official retirement ages, which has been a feature of Swedish policy;
- Secondly, governments could work with employers on schemes to provide training throughout people's working lives which improves employability, upskilling older workers and potentially reducing unemployment of older workers;
- Thirdly, governments could also reduce employment barriers for older workers by tightening regulation around labour market discrimination against older workers.

Source: Adapted from The Golden Age Index (PwC 2016).

Summary

From what used to be a niche area, the role of older workers in the current workscape is widening out to encompass the mainstream. This is driven in the main by business imperatives for the effect it can have on the bottom line but also by an acknowledgement by organisations that inclusion of all demographics in the workforce is open to scrutiny and an issue of corporate social responsibility. For policymakers it is a case for economic growth and sustainability and should relate to issues of social justice.

Against a backdrop of mixed outcomes for policy implementation for older workers, it is pertinent to explore ways to meet the learning needs of older workers to encourage extended working lives across countries where demographic shifts are widely seen. This book originally set out to be a reflection on older worker's learning and their flourishing but has developed into a close scrutiny of diversity and inclusion and older workers' learning as it has become evident that the area of learning cannot be adequately viewed without these lenses.

References

BEIS (2017). *Industrial Strategy – Building a Britain fit for the Future Department for Business, Energy & Industrial Strategy*. www.gov.uk/government/topical-events/the-uks-industrial-strategy [Accessed 27/7/2018]

Boxall, P., and Purcell, J. (2011). *Strategy and Human Resource Management* (3rd edn.). London: Palgrave Macmillan.

Creswell, J.W. (2009). *Research Design: Qualitative, Quantitative, and Mixed Methods Approaches* (3rd edn.). Thousand Oaks, CA: Sage.

Department for Education (DfE) (2017). *Education and Skills Funding Agency*. www.gov.uk/government/organisations/education-and-skills-funding-agency/about [Accessed 20/8/2018]

Department for Work and Pensions (DWP) (2012). *Work Programme*. www.gov.uk/government/collections/work-programme-statistics–2#latest-release [Accessed 21/7/2018].

Department for Work and Pensions (DWP) (2017). *Older Workers and the Workplace Evidence from the Workplace Employment Relations Survey*. Research Report No 939. DWP. www.gov.uk/government/organisations/department-for-work-pensions/about/research#research-publications.

European Association for Education of Adults (EAEA) (2012). *Older Learning – Learning Later in Life*. Policy Paper. www.eaea.org/media/policy-advocacy/eaea-statements/2012_eaea_policy-paper_active-ageing.pdf [Accessed 7/8/2018]

European Commission (2011). *An Agenda for New Skills and Jobs: A European Contribution towards Full Employment*. http://ec.europa.eu/social/main.jsp?catId=958 [Accessed 24/10/2016].

European Commission European Employment Observatory Review (2012). *Employment Policies to Promote Active Ageing*. Luxembourg: Publications Office of the European Union.

European Union (2011). *An Agenda for New Skills and Jobs. A European Contribution Towards Full Employment*. https://publications.europa.eu/en/publication-detail/-/publication/7f39a8c6-068e-434d-a7ce-a9665bf227f9/language-en [Accesssed 27/ 11/ 2018].

Evans, K., Hodkinson, P., and Unwin, L. (Eds.) (2002). *Working to Learn: Transforming Learning in the Workplace*. Abingdon, Oxon: Routledge.

Forbes Insights (2011). *Global Diversity and Inclusion: Fostering Innovation Through a Diverse Workforce*. www.forbes.com/forbesinsights/innovation_diversity/ [Accessed 20/8/2018].

Freire, P. (2005). *Pedagogy of the Oppressed* (30th anniversary edn.). Trans. Myra Bergman Ramos. London: Continuum.

Fukuda-Parr, S., and Shiva Kumar, A.K. (2003). *Readings in Human Development*. Delhi: Oxford University Press.

Gov UK (2012). *Working after State Pension Age*. www.gov.uk/working-retirement-pension-age [Accessed 21/8/2019].

Greller, M.M. (2006). 'Hours invested in professional development during late career as a function of career motivation and satisfaction'. *Career Development International, 11(6)*, 544–559.

Habermas, J. (1987). *The Theory of Communicative Action* (Vol. 2). Trans. T. McCarthy. Cambridge: Polity Press.

Hager, P. (2010). 'Theories of Workplace Learning'. In M. Malloch, L. Cairns, K. Evans and B. O'Connor (Eds.), *The Sage Handbook of Workplace Learning*. London: Sage.

Hunt, V., Prince, S., Dixon-Fyle, S., and Yee, L. (2018). *Delivering through Diversity*. McKinsey & Company. https://www.mckinsey.com/ [Accessed 27/11/2018].

ILO (International Labour Office) (2003). *Key Indicators of the Labour Market*. Geneva: International Labour Organization.

Mayo, P. (2011). 'Series Editor's Preface'. In B. Findsen and M. Formosa (Eds.), *Lifelong Learning in Later Life: A Handbook on Older Adult Learning*. Rotterdam: Sense.

McKinsey & Company (2012). *The World of Work – Jobs, Pay and Skills for 3.5 Billion People*. McKinsey Global Institute. https://www.mckinsey.com/featured-insights/employment-and-growth/the-world-at-work [Accessed 27/ 11/2018].

McKinsey & Company (2015). *Diversity Matters Report*. McKinsey & Company. https://www.mckinsey.com/ [Accessed 27/11/2018].

McNair, S. (2011). *Older People and Skills in a Changing Economy*. London: UK Commission for Employment and Skills.

Moody, H.R., and Sasser, J. (2012). *Ageing: Concepts and Controversies* (7th edn.). Thousand Oaks, CA: Sage.

OECD (2006). *Live Longer Work Longer*. Paris: The Organization for Economic Cooperation and Development (OECD). www.oecd.org/employment/livelongerworklonger.htm [Accessed 8/8/2018].

OECD (2015a). *A Follow-up Assessment Made of the OECD*. 2006 report. OECD.

OECD (2015b). *Ageing and Employment Policies*. Paris: OECD. www.oecd.org/els/emp/ageingandemploymentpolicies.htm [Accessed 4/3/2017].

OECD (2018a). *OECD Employment Outlook 2018*. Paris: OECD. www.oecd.org/els/oecd-employment-outlook-19991266.htm [Accessed 9/8/2018].

OECD (2018b). *OECD Employment Outlook*. UK: OECD. www.oecd.org/united kingdom/publicationsdocuments/reports/ [Accessed 9/8/2018].

Patrickson, M., and Ranzijn, R. (2005). 'Workforce ageing: the challenges for 21st century management'. *International Journal of Organisational Behaviour, 10(4)*, 729–739.

PwC (2016). *Golden Age Index*. PwC. pwc.co.uk/goldenage.

Sen, A. (1993). 'Capability and Well-being'. In M. Nussbaum and A. Sen (Eds.), *The Quality of Life*. Oxford: Clarendon Press.

Tikkanen, T., and Nyhan, B. (Eds.) (2006). *Promoting Lifelong Learning for Older Workers: An International Overview*. Cedefop Reference series 65. The European Centre for the Development of Vocational Training. Luxembourg: Office for Official Publications of the European Communities. www.cedefop.europa.eu/node/11161 [Accessed 22/8/2018].

UNESCO (2015a). *Education 2030. Incheon Declaration and Framework for Action: Towards Inclusive and Equitable Quality Education and Lifelong Learning for All*. http://unesdoc.unesco.org/images/0023/002338/233813M.pdf [Accessed 8/8/2018].

UNESCO (2015b). *Rethinking Education*. https://en.unesco.org/node/270739 [Accessed 8/8/2018].

UNESCO (2015c). *Rethinking Education – Towards a Global Common Good*. Paris: UNESCO.

UNESCO, UNFPA, UNDP, UNHCR, UNICEF, UN Women, & World Bank Group (2015). *Education 2030 – Incheon Declaration – Towards Inclusive and Equitable Quality Education and Lifelong Learning for All*. Incheon, South Korea: UNESCO, UNFPA, UNDP, UNHCR, UNICEF, UN Women and World Bank Group.

United Nations (2015). *Transforming Our World: The 2030 Agenda for Sustainable Development.* http://sustainabledevelopment.un.org [Accessed 20/8/2018].

Unwin, L. (2009). *Connecting Workplace Learning and VET to Lifelong Learning, beyond Current Horizons.* http://citeseerx.ist.psu.edu/viewdoc/download?doi=10.1.1.595.3271&rep=rep1&type=pdf [Accessed 24/10/2016].

World Health Organisation (WHO) (2007). *Global Age-Friendly Cities- A Guide.* www.who.int/ageing/publications/age_friendly_cities_guide/en/ [Accessed 8/8/2018].

2 Learning and development of older workers

Chapter 1 indicated that governments should work with employers on schemes to provide training throughout their working lives to improve employability, increase retention and upskilling of older workers and potentially reduce their unemployment (McNair 2011; Altmann 2014). This would motivate older workers and enable them to stay in the workforce longer which would potentially contribute to a better quality of life in later years (UNESCO 2015). Motivations to learn at older stages of a career are important in shedding light on types of learning and development seen as valuable and valid to both older workers and management.

Therefore, finding ways to meet the learning needs of older workers to encourage extended working lives is pertinent. This chapter explores the major theories of workplace learning and human flourishing, workplace learning connected to lifelong learning for older workers and sustained employability and motivation of older workers.

Links are made between workplace learning and lifelong learning and how it might be further cultivated. Definitions and participation rates in workplace learning are explored. Participation and motivation of older workers in their own learning needs is considered.

Addressing the demographic challenge and employability of older workers in the UK

In the UK, the Age Positive Initiative set up by the Department of Work and Pensions (DWP 2006) to maximise the impact of removing the default retirement age (DRA), works in partnership with business organisations to push for sustained change in employer practices towards increasing the employment and retention of older workers. Over a decade on, there is a growing momentum to encourage employers to consider the value and relevance of older workers. In September 2016, the UK Government appointed a Business Champion for Older Workers and tasked Business in the Community, a UK business-led charity, to support businesses to retain, retrain and recruit older workers. Employers across the UK are being called upon to increase the number of people they employ aged 50–69, by 12% within five years, creating employment opportunities for a million more older workers by 2022.

Theories of workplace learning

Workplace learning [also called work-based learning] "derives its purpose from the context of employment" (Sutherland 1998:5) differing from training restricted to business needs (Evans et al. 2002). Workplace learning is dynamic, covering an expanding variety of elements including business and management thinking, psychology, human resources and industrial relations (Evans et al. 2002). When thinking around learning from a life course perspective, interdisciplinary connections embracing psychological, socio-cultural and postmodern theories (Unwin 2009; Unwin et al. 2015) can deepen our understanding of theories of learning and work (Hager 2004; Unwin 2009; Unwin et al. 2015).

Two workplace learning approaches appear central to a study of older workers and their learning and development. First, a workplace learning approach that includes contextual, socio-cultural, organisational and other factors (Hager 2010). Second, relational and context-related theories, addressing learning relative to the structure and agency debate appear significant. Models of learning which include the role of personal agency (Billett 2001), work agency (Harteis and Goller 2014) and affordances of the workplace which draw attention to those who participate in learning (Billett 2001) also appear to have merit.

Over the last few decades, theoretical understandings of learning have progressed from theories mainly derived from psychological framing where the learner was atomised, individual and human consciousness privileged (Maslow 1970; Rogers and Freiberg 1993), to more complex and multilayered notions of learning to include adult learning, relations, communication, meaning making and identity formation. These developments represent a challenge in focus to arrive at a holistic and more nuanced understanding of later life learning than has been previously suggested (Hager 2010) and they are dynamic.

Theories of workplace learning embrace psychological, socio-cultural and postmodern thinking relating to learning and work, suggests Hager (2010). Contextual factors also play a role in workplace learning. Social, cultural, organisational and other factors, it is argued, have been hitherto underestimated in workplace learning (Baumgartner 2001; Hager 2010) and provide a platform for rethinking the nature of continuing professional learning to better reflect how learning occurs. Furthermore, it has also been suggested that since workplace learning occurs and is embedded in workplace activity and technical and social relations of production (Billett 2001; Hoyrup and Elkjaer 2006; Felstead et al. 2009; Unwin 2009) it is affected by these factors.

The notion of a humanist orientation to learning which is independent of context and where learning is self-actualised and autonomous, as argued by Maslow (1970) and Rogers and Freiberg (1993) is rejected by socio-cultural theory. Vygotsky's theory suggests that we are not separated from contexts in which we live (1978), development for learners "accords with a metaphor of participation" (Hager 2010:23) meaning that we learn through relationships with others.

Evans et al. (2002) also point to dominant literature concerning workplace learning theory, as being broadly in a Vygotsky vein, encompassing situated cognition (Lave and Wenger 1991), or activity theory (Engestrom 2001). Progressing notions centred on socio-cultural theories, Evans et al. (2002) argue that workplace learning literature omits wider social, economic and political factors which would have more resonance to modern public sector and private organisations which are similarly affected by globalisation, government policies and increasing managerialism, forming part of the complexity of what it is to be part of and to manage modern workplaces. Significant in the socio-cultural paradigm, is the relational aspect of learning, being related and interdependent, as well as individual (Billett 2001).

Relational and context-related theories of learning

In what I consider relevant to exploring whether older workers are marginalised when decisions are made with regard to who gets to participate in development, Billett proposes a workplace learning theory which addresses personal agency, arguing for models strengthening relational interdependencies, between individual and social agency, between the engagement of the worker and affordances of the work environment (Billett 2001, 2004, 2008; Billett and Smith 2006). Billett (2001:57) accentuates the subjugation of the individual in socio-cultural theories, where the structuring of "learning experiences in workplaces is directed towards sustaining practice." Complex negotiations about knowledge use, roles and processes occurring between imposed expectation and norms by organisations to further continuity and survival, are set against learners' preferences and goals, "essentially as a question of the learner's participation in situated work activities" (Billett 2004:312).

This development perspective is culture-based influencing what skills people obtain, when they can participate and who is allowed to do which activities (Miller 1993). Touching on inclusion of who is in, and who is out (Slee 2010), it draws our attention to workplace conflict over who participates, relevant in exploring older workers' marginalisation.

Furthermore, as workplaces exist to produce goods and services (Rainbird et al. 2004), they are restricted and affected by a broader productive system and the politico/economic realities they operate within (Ashton 2004; Unwin et al. 2007; Felstead et al. 2009; Unwin 2009). Also, organisations are affected in how they conduct business, time scales, risks taken and opportunities such as who is afforded/chosen for development in a time of cost cutting (Unwin 2009). This is relevant to many sectors affected by increasing competition and the requirement to innovate which has increased exponentially and where, in some countries, public sector organisations receive dwindling government subsidies. As workplaces are sites for learning as Unwin suggests, to improve learning means improving workplace conditions and what happens within workplaces, asking how "we might make greater use of their (employees) potential in order to benefit employers, individuals and society at large" (Unwin 2009:4). This brings in the role of contextual factors and mutual benefit, pertinent in considering to what extent opportunities for development are available, and to whom it is offered in a rapidly changing environment.

Enabling human flourishing in the workplace – theoretical lenses

Billett's reflection on the capability of practitioners, in particular, social practices and their related knowledge domains (Hager 2010), aligns with Sen's work on human flourishing (1993). Sen's work draws on Aristotelian views of what it means to have a good life, "*eudaimonia,*" or human flourishing, where the role of politics is to promote well-being or *eudaimonia* for the populace (Sen 1993). Sen's work operates, or, is *activated* in context. Billett and Sen view the capability of the practitioner, that is the function of the whole person operating in context, an approach that is not humanistic but sociocultural, embedded in context. It is not based on rational choice, but on preferences.

Humanistic theories of learning (Maslow 1943; Rogers 1969, 1983; Rogers and Freiberg 1993), and Knowles' concept of andragogy (1978), view learning as a function of the whole person, being person-centred. Humanistic theories of learning encompass both cognitive and affective domains where self-determination is central. Humanistic psychology is based on beliefs that humans are truly able to decide what they do in their lives, although in reality, this may be difficult to achieve. Workplaces can thwart self-actualisation, curtailing expression and activation of capability, as environmental factors can impede (Sen 1993). Workers are not necessarily free to decide how their learning needs should be met.

Sen's work provides a link to deprivation and exclusion in the workplace, in this case to learning and development. However, there are unintended consequences in that "giving equality in one space frequently leads to inequality in other spaces" (Sen 1992:117) and is open to critique that measuring intangible capabilities for an individual or society are considered difficult (Nussbaum 2003) to effect.

Habermas's theoretical work (1987) on knowledge is relevant as it aligns with Sen's capability approach, being linked to structure and in particular, how spaces might be created to enable older workers' learning. Habermas's (1970, 1987, 1990) critical social theory offers potential in analysing modern workplaces from critical and pragmatic perspectives supporting the role of older workers, including access to equitable training and development. Habermas's writing around emancipation considers how older workers could negotiate what are sometimes unyielding rationalised organisational structures and processes, through spaces where their voice can be heard. This is very pertinent, as an effect of an instrumentalist approach to management and organisations has resulted in rationalisation being the mean ends norm of chasing profitability or targets in contemporary workplaces. So, distribution of life chances of individuals within, or by organisations, can be safely ignored or minimally accommodated through minor or token adjustments in the push for the accepted goal (Adler et al. 2007).

Through a lens of human flourishing, opportunities for development and advancement are anticipated and imagined, staff and management join in a relational and dialectic space to renegotiate, respect and advance older workers' contributions (when not always valued). Presenting an argument for this linkage, an overlap between equality and age is seen. Moody's studies of critical gerontology drawing on Habermas's work (1971), challenge predominant views of ageing arguing a type of "emancipatory knowledge" offering "a positive vision of how things might be different or what a rationally defensible vision of a 'good old age' might be is absent" (Moody 1993:xvii). This view turns ageing on its head, with older people staking a rightful claim in the workplace, re-envisioning learning spaces for older workers and career progression.

For Habermas (1971:290), human interests circulate around three "knowledge interests": technical control relating to labour activity, but humans should not be diminished by it; interest in mutual understanding linked to interaction in the lifeworld and communicative action; and emancipation from domination in "the sense of being in control of the conditions under which one lives" (ibid.). Where the first two interests are linked to labour and language, the interest in emancipation is linked to power. Habermas examined possibilities to survive in increasingly rationalised societies, proposing a reconceptualisation of modernity not as a negative factor but:

> The development of communicative rationality, practical reason (Kant), the freeing of morality from its religious base (Durkheim) and the emergence of the mature individual (Mead and Kohlberg).
>
> (Rasmussen in Rasmussen and Swindal 2002:232)

Teasing out notions of emancipation, Chapter 3 explores the findings of a study into a higher education workplace which considers whether Habermas's Theory of Communicative Action (TCA) (1984), as a counterpoint to rationalisation in society, could be applied to micro levels of the workplace, specifically older workers' development opportunities. Habermas (1990) viewed dialogic spaces as a mechanism for workers' agency in rationalised organisations, and in this case, spaces for dialogue for older workers to be agentic. Discovering "voice" in lived experiences of older age, we can begin to consider what an emancipatory perspective would be for older workers in contemporary workplaces. Habermas's work (1971, 1987) on rationalisation and modernity, the replacement of traditions, values and emotions which motivate society, to ones based on rational and calculated ideas, were influenced by Weber's "iron cage" where humans lose their individualism, trapped in a rules-based rational world (Finlayson 2005:56,140).

For Habermas, rationalisation is problematic, its remedy being rationalisation of communicative action through social interaction, leading to communication free from domination; free and open communication (Habermas 1970:290–292). The TCA (1984) viewed humans not colonised by the "lifeworld" of the system, but free to be capable of critical thinking and political action. The TCA is defined as "actors in society seeking to reach common understanding and to coordinate actions by reasoned argument, consensus and cooperation rather than strategic action strictly in pursuit of their own goals" (Habermas 1984:286), implying a groundswell of similar, communitarian thinking or norms. Based on pragmatism and communicative action, rather than critique of modernity, implying a critical view of the technical rationality, it creates and allows preconditions for a paradigm shift on rationality (Englund 2006). Habermas saw its realisation through "ideal speech situations" (ISS); the importance of linguistic communication in coming together seeking agreement on important issues, through informed discourse in a sphere of public debate, such as education (Englund 2006). Rasmussen discussed Habermas's reconceptualisation:

> Language as a communicative discourse is emancipatory (p.18) and his task is to rehabilitate the project of modernity by reconstructing it viz a viz the theory of communication, that is communicative action, communicative reason (p.4).
>
> (Rasmussen and Swindal 2002:12)

Thus, the TCA can be viewed as a theory of integration (Englund 2006), having potential to make Habermas's work relevant to workplaces, providing a theoretical basis for a view of development and learning, transcending bureaucracy and market-driven climates. Chapter 3 provides an example of the potential for this theory of integration in a discussion of the findings of a study into a UK university.

However, Habermas's theories have been critiqued as wide-ranging, difficult and overcomplex (Finlayson 2005), for an overemphasis on the language and of being unduly theoretical and systematic (Terry 1997). Furthermore, Ritzer (2012) suggests that forces in the modern world which distort the free speech process, preventing an emergence of consensus must be overcome to realise Habermas's rationalised, ideal society. Nevertheless, it is also argued such criticism is misconceived; the theories provide "original, insightful and thoughtful responses to alienation and social fragmentation afflicting modern society" (Finlayson 2005:58). Habermas's work is functional not moral or ethical. Its purpose is functional, as colonisation "thwarts the good functioning of the lifeworld depriving society of the benefits of communication and discourse found in shared meanings and attitudes, feelings of belonging, social order and other areas" (ibid:58). Whether Habermas's implementation and practice of ISS was tested is unclear. Despite criticisms, ISS related to organisations could shed light on an exploration of older workers in modern society, approached from a pragmatic perspective, to align the systems structure and the everyday lifeworld of older workers to achieve an engaged, active and fulfilled workforce.

Barnett (2012:3), imagining future possibilities for 21st century universities but also of relevance to many contemporary workplace settings, discusses Habermasian views of a university reflective of ideal speech situations. Although critical of Habermas's lack of insight of modern universities' complexity, Barnett proposed a redesign of the university encompassing a "multi-planar" approach, reaching into and opening up spaces for intellectual collaborative thinking, and imagining of possibilities. Preconditions include an ethos of trust and communicative openness, where "something approaching a Habermasian ideal speech situation is logically entailed, and where hierarchy and boundaries need to be temporarily set aside" (ibid.), supporting requirements for Sen's flourishing vectors *in situ* for flourishing to occur in all staff, including older workers.

Workplace learning and connection to lifelong learning

Exploring how much older workers' learning takes place is valid as workplaces are important sites for learning in knowledge-based economies, and there is evidence that age matters in opportunities given for professional development and training, with those under 30 most likely to benefit (SSDA 2007). As ever more learning is through work, finding out what types of workplace learning offer a "best fit" for older workers and environments they best learn in is important for flourishing, and can be mutually beneficial to workers and employers.

It is argued that the increasing tendency for individuals to fuse the working and nonworking parts and spaces of their lives (Field 2006; Felstead et al. 2009) raises questions 'as to the extent to which "learning at, through and for work" is embedded in lifelong learning as opposed to being separated from it' (Unwin 2009:2). Similarly, others argue for expanded notions of work-based learning reflecting learning at work, for work and through work, arguing work-based learning expands and develops wider capabilities, self-esteem and professional identity (Evans et al. 2010:159) encompassing career progression either within the same organisation or externally.

Recognising the conjunct between individual and social structures and models of learning, Hodkinson et al. (2004) consider that links between workplace learning and lifelong learning are present when there is acknowledgement that people can be identified as being both separate from their workplace and incorporated into it. They propose people's view of learning might take on a lifelong learning perspective, drawing attention to how identities and individual biographies are significant in learning, as people have lives outside of work and lives which predate their working spaces. This shapes how people view themselves in their learning and how they approach it, suggesting a role for individual growth which may not be restricted by or reduced by social constructs, such as age.

Models of workplace learning include learning with and through work (Billett 2001, 2010; Unwin 2009) and work-process knowledge (Boreham et al. 2002). Billett (2001, 2010) makes the case for understanding learning as participation, where learning is proposed as being interdependent between the individual and the social practice. Billett (2004) argues that considering learning as participation in work is important when lifelong learning policies and practices (OECD 1998) pass the responsibility for maintaining currency increasingly to workers. Participation in learning becomes ever more crucial proposes Billett (2001), when for the majority of workers, the workplace represents the only or most viable location to learn and/or develop vocational practice. In what is a complex theoretical field, this model argues that lifelong learning can occur through and at work, emphasising the role of work practices and learning, including informal learning (Billett 2004).

Boreham et al. (2002) too consider that the social aspects of learning support the building/creation of work-process knowledge, defined as knowledge that an employee needs to work flexibly in modern workplaces. Knowledge comes from the collective memories of the individuals in a community of practice, and in the artefacts and technology within them. Part of what it means to have work process knowledge is to be able to work collaboratively, where members of a community share knowledge in the practice of their work to carry out tasks and working roles. Language enables workers to construct knowledge in the workplace, learning perspectives are carried forward in language that reflects organisational culture structure (Boreham 2004). What appears critical then is how the workplace is managed, accentuating the role of cultural and organisational structures in understanding processes of organisational learning.

Workplaces offering employees learning are important sites not just for learning, but in mediating flourishing in the immediate environment and society, extending learning to life course perspectives. Workplace learning is fundamental for individual learning, but more widely, where individuals are part of a learning society. According to UNESCO (Faure et al. 1972), a learning society is viewed as the involvement of society as participant and actor in education and whose community can engage in critical dialogue and actions (Coffield 1997). The UNESCO report "The Treasure Within" (Delors 1996) positioned education as central to a nation's economic development, considering that education should extend beyond formal learning into informal learning, expanding on the notion of lifelong learning. The OECD Knowledge Management in the Learning Society (2000), in developing the 1972 UNESCO framework (Faure et al. 1972), advocated for a learning society and the contribution that lifelong learning can make to human development.

Definitions of lifelong learning are myriad and contested, recognising learning may be conducted over a lifespan (Field 2006), and deliberate learning over a person's lifetime (Knapper and Cropley 2000). Given the relative shortness of compulsory schooling it can be argued much learning is in the workplace. Two competing paradigms of lifelong learning have been driven by UNESCO and OECD over the last 40 years. One, a wider holistic view of human development, the other a functionalist view of human capital. The Learning to Be Report (UNESCO 1972) emphasised the right to fulfil individual potential, personal development through lifelong education. Social inclusivity amidst "the variety of nations and cultures, of political options and degrees of development" (ibid:v) was recognised as a key principle in the report. However, lifelong learning has become part of the economic and political discourse of global capitalism for increasing competitive performance, positioning people as human resources, discarded and retrained if their job is redundant (Jarvis 2001). The emphasis is firmly on economic rationales where "lifelong learning from early childhood education to active learning in retirement will be an important factor in promoting employment and economic development" (OECD 1997:13). Nevertheless, there is mutual benefit and value between learning for personal development and learning for organisational benefit to realise organisational imperatives seen in the shaded part of the overlapping circles in Figure 2.1, which could convey spaces for ideal speech situations. Spaces could be provided for learning through the concept of lifewide learning (Skolverket 2000; Clark 2005) which considers that learning occurs in different places simultaneously and is helpful in widening out where learning can occur. The term lifewide learning (Jackson 2008), embraces the many sites for learning that occur in a learner's life at any point in time with work being a very important context but not the only one (ibid.). Lifewide

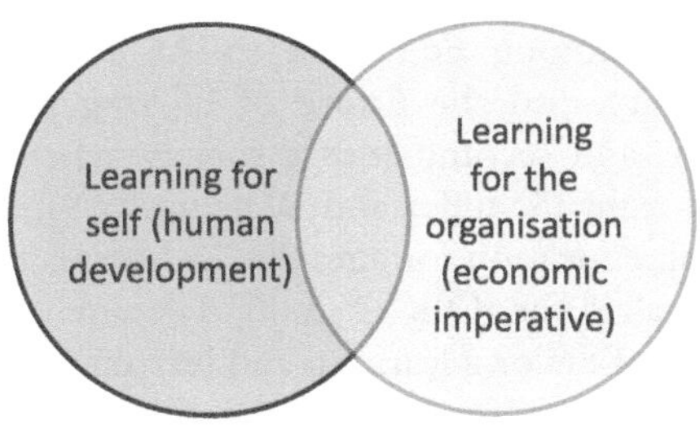

Fig 2.1 Focus of learning in the workplace

learning "acknowledges the shift from traditional stable structures of learning to more fluid, transient and technology-enabled structures of the 21st century" (Jackson 2011:xii), which offers opportunities for holistic learning at work.

Barnett (2010) proposes that there is learning across an individual's lifeworld at any moment in time in learning spaces that may be completely different from one another. Critically, these learning experiences will be marked by differences of power, ownership, visibility, sharedness, cost and recognition. Crucially, both lifelong and lifewide learning imply a shift in responsibility for education and learning from the public to the private and civil spheres (Skolverket 2000). Nevertheless, it is argued that it is still the responsibility of government and society to create good conditions for lifelong and lifewide learning, particularly by promoting educational equity (ibid.), which has inferences for older workers who are not always first in line for development. Similar to lifelong learning, lifewide learning is connected to both formal and informal learning and requires the capabilities to plan, manage and self-regulate own learning and development. These capacities will be key to being an effective and agentic learner where personalisation, collaboration and informalisation (informal learning) will be at the core of learning in the future (Redecker et al. 2011).

In connecting lifelong and workplace learning, the OECD (Kallen and Bengtsson 1973) proposes that the concept of "recurrent education" entails regular participation across the life course to nurture career and skills development. Morgan-Klein and Osborne (2007:2) suggest that this concept is related "to human capital theory which emphasises the value of investing in education and training since this is assumed to bring returns in economic development and growth for individuals and for society."

Links to lifelong learning are present if it is accepted people are separate from their workplace and incorporated into it (Hodkinson et al. 2004). Lifelong learning plays a role in transforming lives. For Dewey, individual growth is intrinsic in how society should view its members, and growth has a moral dimension (1938:114). Allied to Dewey's moral dimension, what differentiates "doing" from "learning" is that the latter changes what we are by changing our ability to participate, belong and negotiate meaning (Wenger 1998:226), highlighting the transformative and moral dimension to learning, its role for flourishing in society and in the workplace. The England and Wales National Institute of Adult Continuing Education (NIACE) (now the Learning and Work Institute) enquiry into the future of lifelong learning recognises this transformative power, and recommends a society where learning plays a full role, being a human right (Schuller and Watson 2009). The enquiry supports enhanced training and education for ages 50–75. Access to up-to-date skills for older people, is also called for (OECD 2006; Tikkanen and Nyhan 2006).

However, concepts of lifelong learning and learning at work are problematic due to scepticism about how much learning occurs. Workplaces as learning environments are evident in research and policy but rarely discussed relative to lifelong learning (Unwin 2009). With workplaces crucially important sites for learning and access to learning (Evans et al. 2002), inherent is the recognition of power differences and who gets to participate in this learning. These restrictions limit the political and philosophical moral ideals of UNESCO's Faure report (Faure et al. 1972); reframing the original ideal to lifelong learning, dominantly linked to training and new skills, for rapidly changing workplaces (Matheson and Matheson 1996; Bagnall 2000).

Power differentials and workplace climate can work for or against older workers, providing expansive or restrictive learning environments and motivation to engage in learning. Learning can be limited through workplace structure, power, gender relations and culture (Rainbird et al. 2004). Belatedly, age as a limiting factor, has been recognised. Bringing the two concepts of older workers and lifelong learning together (previously separate discourses), Tikkanen and Nyhan (2006) draw on empirical research across Europe, Australia, Japan and the US, stressing that the demographic challenge affects everybody in society as everyone eventually grows old, so age-management, lifelong learning and training measures that anticipate people's needs at different life phases, needs implementing in all workplaces. However, for lifelong learning to become a reality for older workers "ordinary workplaces must become primary places of learning," which again raises important issues about employers' roles in promoting lifelong learning (ibid:3).

Participation and motivation of older workers in learning

Nevertheless, Hager (2004) argues that pockets of "good" lifelong learning are still found in reduced circumstances or "alienation" (Dewey 1916). Dewey recognised workplace constraints, proposing that by viewing learning differently as a process rather than product, it was possible to hone meanings about socio-political aspects of work extending beyond workplaces, sharpening an educational experience of working, connecting to workplace learning. Work and lifelong learning are "occupation as becoming" as workers place high value on satisfaction obtained from work giving a strong sense of personal development. This provided intrinsic satisfaction, separate from work and workplaces that may reduce motivation (Dewey 1916) and potentially relevant to older workers. If work, as Dewey suggested, is "creativity" rather than "labour," it is possible to see lifelong learning *through* and *at work* possible. Such learning emphasises the role of work practices and learning, including informal learning, becoming ever more crucial when, as mentioned earlier, participation in workplace learning is sometimes the only location where workers can develop their lifelong learning and ability to flourish in work and beyond (Billett 2001).

Providing appropriate training and development opportunities over the life course will be crucial in maintaining healthy and productive lives; encouraging lifelong learning and importantly participation can lead to increased employability for the 50+ cohort. Conversely, it is this same cohort that is most unlikely to participate in work, possibly falling to 0% by 2025 for the 65+ age group (Hyde and Phillipson 2014). A policy brief commissioned by the UK Commission for Employment and Skills, bringing together research on equity and employment for those disadvantaged in the UK labour market, indicates participation rates are lowest and fall steepest for ages 60–69 years (McNair 2011), with serious inferences for this older segment of the workforce in the UK. Additionally, poor employability is a key challenge in increasing employment rates of those 50+ (ibid.). Adopting age-friendly employment policies and practices to reverse the negative effects of older people on public finance can "convert the process of population ageing to one of being an opportunity for society and older workers" (OECD 2006:8). Cedefop's EU commissioned (2006) overview of contributions from scholars in Europe, Australia, Japan and the US into older workers and lifelong learning indicates that age-friendly workplace learning practices should include improved access to up-to-date skills, employment services and improved working conditions (Tikkanen and Nyhan 2006).

Findsen and Formosa (2011:117) argue motivation always underpins participation, raising two questions. What motivates those for later life learning? How might age affect workplace motivation? The findings of the NIACE UK Adult Participation in Learning Survey (NIACE 2015a), an annual survey series, provides an overview of the level of participation in learning by adults with a breakdown of who participates and who does not. The survey adopts a broad definition of learning, including formal, nonformal and informal learning. From a poll of 5,000 adults aged 17 and over across the four UK nations, it appears a fifth of adults (22%) were learning at that time, with around 41% having taken part in some form of learning in the previous three years, although a third of adults (33%) had not participated in learning since leaving full-time education. Although the 2015 survey indicated that overall participation in learning had increased slightly after remaining the same for the previous three years, "there has been little variation in the overall level of participation since the survey began in 1996" (ibid:1).

The findings of this same study indicate that engagement in learning in the UK is unevenly distributed and is determined by social class, employment status, age and prior learning. Older age groups are less likely to participate in learning, with a decline in participation for those aged 55+, with only 31% of those aged 55–64, 20% of those aged 65–74 and 12% of those aged 75+ considering themselves as learners (ibid:4).

The most commonly cited reasons within the 2010 National Adult Learner Survey (BIS 2012) for not learning are cost (58%), lack of time (42%), and inability to fit learning around job (29%), or family life (25%) 2010 National Adult Learner Survey (BIS 2010). The 2010 survey which covered England only, conducted 4,647 interviews with 16–24 year olds not in continuous full-time education and those aged 25 and over. Uncovering motivations to learn, respondents were also asked to consider what would motivate them to take part in learning. Three in five (62%) were motivated by the prospect of learning something new and two in five were motivated by improved job prospects and income (mentioned by 42% each). Motivations for learning were closely related to life stages. Respondents aged 16–39 were particularly motivated by enhanced job prospects (promotion and higher income), while those in the latter stages of their working life wanted to be able to improve their performance at work for their own job satisfaction. People aged 20–49 wanted to learn to help their children, while those aged 50 and over placed greater value on learning new things, meeting new people and confidence building (ibid.). Conversely, nonparticipation in learning had negative implications for this grouping's employability, well-being, resilience and furthering of intellectual possibility (ibid:2012).

The powerful relationship between learning and work is evident across the NIACE survey (BIS 2012). Adults in work are more likely than those outside of the workplace to take part in learning. Nearly four-fifths of learners surveyed say that they took up learning for work-related reasons (ibid.).

The economic prosperity of countries also depends on people becoming more skilled, innovative and capable through continuing to learn. Thus, it appears critical to understand what types of workplace learning participation might be mutually beneficial to increase employee engagement and organisational well-being. Costley and Critten (2012) surveying graduates, suggest that high-work level thinking skills are needed in future workforces and developed through applying learning and reflecting on real work issues. Practically, these skills can be developed through researching aspects of their workplace, developing key skills for understanding research statistics, improving presentation skills and conveying learning to others. Developing such skills sets are also relevant to older workers.

What motivates older workers?

Kanfer and Ackerman (2004) argue that ageing and adult development represent important but largely unexplored influences on work motivation. Their integrative framework for the use and effectiveness of different motivational strategies with midlife and older workers in a variety of jobs located motivation in the broader context of lifespan research which emphasises four intraindividual change trajectories over the life course (loss, gain, reorganization and exchange). This framework for learning suggests work circumstances affect work motivation aligning with socio-contextual learning theories. Practically, Kanfer and Ackerman argue work motivation may be improved by organisational strategies and managerial practices taking account normative patterns of adult development (ibid.). This argument was reinforced through a meta-analysis of 24 empirical and nine conceptual studies (those sampled were all from Western developed countries) showing most age-related factors can impact negatively on motivation for extended working lives, most significantly declining health and career plateaus, which should be addressed through human resource management policies and practices including ergonomic adjustments and continuous career development (Kooij et al. 2013).

Theories of work motivation (Herzberg 1959; McClelland 1961; Vroom 1964) may be limited in understanding older workers' motivations and organisation practices, tending to focus on intrinsic rewards related to learning and emphasise extrinsic rewards around pay, promotion and recognition. Conversely, Kanfer and Ackerman's study found that learning and extrinsic rewards are often constrained for older workers leading to them being less valued (Kanfer and Ackerman 2004). Furthermore, knowledge utilisation, helping, collaboration and enhancing positive affect, seen as motivators, are not addressed in either theory or practice (ibid.) partially borne out by some evidence of a lack of enthusiasm of the over 55s in learning new skills (ibid.). This lack of enthusiasm shown was consistent with a meta-analysis of 418 empirical studies relating to age stereotypes of older workers in the US indicating that older workers were less willing to participate in training and career development (in contrast to Greller's 2006 findings). However, the findings disproved other common stereotypical views of older workers (Ng and Feldman 2012:824). Moreover, a comparison of national Austrian labour force data with EU labour force survey data (ELS 2008) tracking participation in training indicated closeness to retirement led to a decrease in training participation but chronological age was not related to training across the age groups sampled, leading to difficulties in finding a straightforward relationship between training and ageing (Schmidt 2010).

It appears that what motivates older workforces is multilayered, requiring playing close attention to the "complex interplay of educational level, occupational status, company environments (provision of time and cost incentives for the employee as well as sector-specific differences in training needs) and individual cost-benefit considerations" in terms of how decisions are made to participate in training (Schmidt 2010:211). Care needs to be taken in not falling back on negative stereotypical views of older workers to decipher what is really occurring as the influences of stereotypes and their role in workplace culture is significant to understanding how organisations treat different groups of workers (Unwin et al. 2015). Rather more, we should direct attention to the "heterogeneity of older workers and the organisations in which they work" (Schmidt 2010:211) where a more holistic response to workforce development is required which may not be about counting days participating in training or the number of qualifications a person obtains (Unwin et al. 2015).

A UK-wide study of 1615 participants aged 18–55+, showed the perceived importance of learning new skills, which is different to a lack of enthusiasm, fell with age compared with 18–24 younger age groups (AAT 2015).[1] However, even though the perceived importance fell corresponding with age, it does not necessarily follow that it would be lower amongst those aged 55+. The research suggests this is probably because once a person reaches the top of their career they feel that additional skills will add little job security. An additional factor is that often those researched had been in their current occupation for several decades and may feel that they have mastered the most important skills. This mindset leads to a lower uptake of training. Contrastingly, aligned to the aforementioned 2010 National Adult Learner Survey (2012) and the findings of Kooij et al. (2008), life transitions were a motivator for later life learning. Work-related reasons included sustaining employment, making existing work more enjoyable, facilitating career change, providing greater financial security and gaining job specific skills or qualifications (Findsen and McCullough 2006). Empirical studies show the importance of training needs being relevant as older workers are more critical consumers of training products (CEDEFOP 2008), with "buy in" difficult to achieve if no value or benefit was seen.

These empirical studies are helpful in moving towards some understanding of what motivates older workers' participation in learning as they rely on large scale nationally representative samples, which encompass older workers' experience of learning across a range of sectors.

Summary

If as argued, workplaces are significant for lifelong learning and as sites of learning, how might we make the most use of older workers' potential to benefit individuals and employers in wider society, thereby recognising learning is a human right and education a form of democracy (Dewey 1916)? Obtaining an answer means exploring what learning older workers value, what learning employers value and how any differing views on what should be offered be reconciled between these two groupings, which is taken up in the findings of a pragmatic higher education workplace study in the next chapter.

Note

1 A YouGov online survey conducted for AAT with a total sample size of 1615 adults, in February 2015. Covering all areas of Great Britain, across all vocational and professional sectors, the results were weighted to be representative of all adults in Great Britain (aged 18+).

References

AAT (Association of Accounting Technicians) (2015). *The Economic Benefits of Adults Reskilling*. London: Centre for Economics and Business Research Ltd (CEBR).

Adler, P.S., Forbes, L.C., and Willmott, H. (2007). '3 critical management studies'. *The Academy of Management Annals*, *1(1)*, 119–179.

Altmann, R. (2014). *A New Vision for Older Workers: Retain, Retrain and Recruit*. London: Department for Work and Pensions.

Ashton, D. (2004). 'The impact of organisational structure and practices on learning in the workplace'. *International Journal of Training and Development*, *8(1)*, 43–53.

Bagnall, R. (2000). 'Lifelong learning and the limitations of economic determinism'. *International Journal of Lifelong Education, 19(1)*, 20–35.

Barnett, R. (2010). Life-wide Education: A new and transformative concept for higher education. In N. J. Jackson and R.K. Law, (Eds.), *Enabling a More Complete Education: Encouraging, recognising and Enabling a More Complete Education Conference e-Proceedings.* http://lifewidelearningconference.pbworks.com/w/page/24285296/E%20proceedings [Accessed 28/11/2018].

Barnett, R. (2012). *Imagining the University*. Abingdon, Oxon: Routledge.

Baumgartner, L. (2001). 'Four Adult Development Theories and Their Implications for Practice'. In *Focus on the Basics, Adult Development*, Vol. 5 (B), 29–34. National Center for the Study of Adult Learning and Literacy (NCSALL). www.ncsall.net/index.html@id=481.html [Accessed 24/1/2018].

Billett, S. (2001). 'Participation and continuity at work: a critique of current workplace learning discourses'. *Context, Power and Perspective: Confronting the Challenges to Improving Attainment in Learning at Work.* Joint Network/SKOPE/TLRP International workshop 8–10th November, Northampton: Sunley Management Centre, University College of Northampton. www.infed.org/archives/e-texts/billett_workplace_learning [Accessed 15/2/2018].

Billett, S. (2004). 'Workplace participatory practices: conceptualising workplaces as learning environments'. *Journal of Workplace Learning, 16(6)*, 312–324.

Billett, S. (2008). 'Learning throughout working life: a relational interdependence between personal and social agency'. *British Journal of Educational Studies, 56(1)*, 39–58.

Billett, S. (2010). 'Subjectivity, Self and Personal Agency in Learning thorough and for Work'. In M. Malloch, L. Cairns, K. Evans and B. O'Connor (Eds.), *The Sage Handbook of Workplace Learning*. London: Sage.

Billett, S. and Smith, R. (2006). 'Personal Agency and Epistemology at Work'. In S. Billett, T. Fenwick and M. Somerville (Eds.), *Work Subjectivity and Learning – Understanding Learning through Working Life.* Dordrecht, The Netherlands: Springer.

Boreham, N. (2004). 'A theory of collective competence: challenging the neo-liberal individualisation of performance at work'. *British Journal of Educational Studies, 52(1)*, 5–17.

Boreham, N., Fischer, M., and Samurçay, R. (Eds.). (2002). *Work Process Knowledge.* London: Routledge.

CEDEFOP (The European Centre for the Development of Vocational Training) (2008). *Validation of Non-formal and Informal Learning in Europe- A Snapshot.* European Centre for the Development of Vocational Training (CEDEFOP). www.cedefop.europa.eu/files/4073_en.pdf [Accessed 2/6/2018].

Clark, T. (2005). 'Lifelong, life-wide or life sentence?' *Australian Journal of Adult Learning, 45(1)*, 47–62.

Coffield, F. (Ed.). (1997). *A National Strategy for Lifelong Learning* (ED 419 878). Newcastle upon Tyne: Newcastle University.

Costley, C., and Critten, P. (2012). 'The business value of structured workplace learning'. *Global Focus Magazine, 6(1)*, 14–17. http://issuu.com/efmd/docs/gf-special-vol-06-issue [Accessed 24/10/2016].

Delors, J. (1996). *Learning: The Treasure within.* Report to UNESCO of the International Commission on Education for the Twenty-First Century. Paris, France: UNESCO Publishing.

Department for Business, Innovation and Skills (BIS) (2010). *National Adult Learner Survey*, https://www.gov.uk/government/publications/national-adult-learner-survey-2010. [Accessed 29/11/2018].

Department for Business, Innovation and Skills (BIS) (2012). *National Adult Learner Survey 2010*. BIS Research paper number 63. London: BIS.
Department of Work and Pensions (DWP) (2006). *The Age Positive Initiative*. www.gov.uk/government/collections/age-positive [Accessed 4/7/2018].
Dewey, J. (1916). *Democracy and Education: An Introduction to Philosophy of Education*. Basingstoke: Macmillan.
Dewey, J. (1938). *Experience and Education*. Indianapolis, IN: Kappa. D.P. Publications. www.gutenberg.org/files/852/852-h/852-h.htm#link2HCH0023 [Accessed 15/5/2018].
Engestrom, Y. (2001). 'Expansive learning at work: toward an activity theoretical reconceptualization'. *Journal of Education and Work, 14(1)*, 133–156.
Englund, T. (2006). 'Deliberative communication: a pragmatist proposal'. *Journal of Curriculum Studies, 38(5)*, 503–520.
European Union (2008). *European Labour Force Survey*, Eurostat https://ec.europa.eu/eurostat/en/web/products-statistical-working-papers/-/KS-RA-10-005 [Accessed 29/11/2018].
Evans, K., Guile, D., and Harris, J. (2010). 'Rethinking Work-Based Learning – For Education Professionals and Professionals Who Educate'. In M. Malloch, L. Cairns, K. Evans and B. O'Connor (Eds.), *The Sage Handbook of Workplace Learning*. London: Sage.
Evans, K., Hodkinson, P., and Unwin, L. (2002). (Eds.). *Working to Learn: Transforming Learning in the Workplace*. Abingdon, Oxon: Routledge.
Faure, E., Herrera, F., Kaddoura, A.-R., Lopes, H., Petrovsky, A.V., Rahnema, M., and Ward, F.C. (1972). *Learning to Be Report – The World of Education Today and Tomorrow*. UNESCO. http://unesdoc.unesco.org/images/0000/000018/001801e.pdf [Accessed 13/5/2018].
Felstead, A., Fuller, A., Jewson, J., and Unwin, L.K. (2009). *Improving Working for Learning*. Abingdon, Oxon: Routledge.
Field, J. (2006). *Lifelong Learning and the New Educational Order*. London: Trentham Books.
Findsen, B., and McCullough, S. (2006). *Older Adults' Engagement with Further and Higher Education in the West of Scotland: Tracking Educational Journeys*. www.researchgate.net/publication/237834214_Older_Adults%27_Engagement_with_Further_and_Higher_Education_in_the_West_of_Scotland_Tracking_Educational_Journeys
Findsen, B., and Formosa, M. (2011). *Lifelong Learning in Later Life: A Handbook on Older Adult Learning*. Rotterdam: Sense.
Finlayson, J.G. (2005). *Habermas – A Very Short Introduction*. Oxford: Oxford.
Greller, M.M. (2006). 'Hours invested in professional development during late career as a function of career motivation and satisfaction'. *Career Development International, 11(6)*, 544–559.
Habermas, J. (1970). *Towards a Rational Society*. Boston: Beacon Press.
Habermas, J. (1971). *Knowledge and Human Interests*. Trans. J.J. Shapiro. London: Polity Press.
Habermas, J. (1984). *The Theory of Communicative Action* (Vol. I). Boston: Beacon Press.
Habermas, J. (1987). *The Theory of Communicative Action* (Vol. 2, Trans. T. McCarthy). Cambridge: Polity Press.
Habermas, J. (1990). *Moral Consciousness and Communicative Action*. Cambridge: Polity Press.
Hager, P. (2004). 'Front-loading, workplace learning and skill development'. *Educational Philosophy and Theory, 36(5)*, 523–534.
Hager, P. (2010). 'Theories of Workplace Learning'. In M. Malloch, L. Cairns, K. Evans and B. O'Connor (Eds.), *The Sage Handbook of Workplace Learning*. London: Sage.

Harteis, C., and Goller, M. (2014). 'New Skills for New Jobs: Work Agency as a Necessary Condition for Successful Lifelong Learning'. In T. Halttunen, M. Koivisto and S. Billett (Eds.), *Promoting, Assessing, Recognizing and Certifying Lifelong Learning – International Perspectives and Practices*. Dordrecht: Springer.

Herzberg, F. (1959). *Two Factor Theory*. www.netmba.com/mgmt/ob/motivation/herzberg/ [Accessed 24/8/2018].

Hodkinson, P., Hodkinson, H., Evans, K., Kersh, N., Fuller, A., Unwin, L., and Senker, P. (2004). 'The significance of individual biography in workplace learning'. *Studies in the Education of Adults, 36(1)*, 6–25.

Hoyrup, S., and Elkjaer, B. (2006). 'Reflection: Taking It Beyond the Individual'. In D. Boud, P. Cressey and P. Docherty (Eds.), *Productive Reflection at Work*. Abingdon, Oxon: Routledge.

Hyde, M., and Phillipson, C. (2014). *How Can Lifelong Learning, Including Continuous Training within the Labour Market, Be Enabled and Who Will Pay for This? Looking Forward to 2025 and 2040 How Might This Evolve?* Foresight, Government Office for Science.

Jackson, N.J. (2008). *A Life-Wide Curriculum: Enriching a Traditional WIL Scheme through New Approaches to Experience-Based Learning*. Proceedings of the WACE Symposium Sydney 2008. www.acen.edu.au/images/resources/conferences/wace_conference_08/eproceedings.pdf [Accessed 27/3/2018].

Jackson, N.J. (2011). *Learning for a Complex World: A Lifewide Concept of Learning, Education and Personal Development*. Indiana: Author House.

Jarvis, P. (2001). *Learning in Later Life: An Introduction for Educators and Carers*. London: Kogan Page.

Kallen, D., and Bengtsson, J. (1973). *Recurrent Education: A Strategy for Lifelong Learning*. Paris: Centre for Educational Research and Innovation. Organisation for Economic Cooperation and Development (OECD).

Kanfer, R., and Ackerman, P.L. (2004). 'Aging, adult development, and work motivation'. *Academy of Management Review, 29(3)*, 440–458.

Knapper, C., and Cropley, J. (2000). *Lifelong Learning in Higher Education* (3rd edn.). London: Kogan Page.

Knowles, M.S. (1978). *The Adult Learner: A Neglected Species* (2nd edn.). Houston: Gulf Pub. Co., Book Division.

Kooij, D., de Lange, A., Jansen, P., and Dikkers, J. (2008). 'Older workers' motivation to continue to work: five meanings of age: a conceptual review'. *Journal of Managerial Psychology, 23(4)*, 364–394.

Kooij, D.T.A.M., Guest, D.E., Clinton, M., Knight, T., Jansen, P.G.W., and Dikkers, J.S.E. (2013). 'How the impact of HR practices on employee well-being and performance changes with age'. *Human Resource Management Journal, 23*, 18–35. doi:10.1111/1748-8583.12000

Lave, J., and Wenger, E. (1991). *Situated Learning: Legitimate Peripheral Participation*. Cambridge: Cambridge University Press.

Maslow, A.H. (1943). 'A theory of human motivation'. *Psychological Review, 50(4)*, 370-396.

Maslow, A.H. (1970). *Motivation and Personality*. New York: Harper and Row.

Matheson, D., and Matheson, C. (1996). 'Lifelong learning and lifelong education: a critique'. *Research in Post-Compulsory Education, 1(2)*, 219–236.

McClelland, D. (1961). *The Achieving Society*. Princeton, NJ: D.Van Nostrand.

McNair, S. (2011). *Older People and Skills in a Changing Economy*. London: UK Commission for Employment and Skills.

Miller, P. (1993). *Theories of Developmental Psychology* (3rd edn.). New York: W. H. Freeman.

Moody, H.R. (1993). 'Overview: What Is Critical Gerontology and Why Is It Important?' In T.R. Cole, W.A. Achenbaum, P.L. Jakobi and R. Kastenbaum (Eds.), *Voices and Visions of Aging: Toward a Critical Gerontology*. New York: Springer.

Morgan-Klein, B., and Osborne, M. (2007). *The Concepts and Practices of Lifelong Learning*. Abingdon, Oxon: Routledge.

Ng, T.W.H., and Feldman, D.C. (2012). 'Evaluating six common stereotypes about older workers with meta-analytical data'. *Personnel Psychology, 65(4)*, 821–858.

NIACE (2015a). *Adult Participation in Learning Survey*. Learning and Work Institute. www.learningandwork.org.uk/resource/2015-adult-participation-in-learning-survey/ [Accessed 16/7/2018].

NIACE (2015b). *Extending Working Life through Career Review at Mid-life*. Leicester: NIACE.

Nussbaum, M. (2003). 'Capabilities as fundamental entitlements: Sen and Social Justice'. *Feminist Economics, 9(2–3)*, 33–59.

OECD (1997). *Lifelong Learning for All*. Paris: The Organization for Economic Cooperation and Development (OECD).

OECD (1998). *Lifelong Learning: A Monitoring Framework and Trends in Participation. Educational Policy Analysis*. Paris: The Organization for Economic Cooperation and Development (OECD).

OECD (2000). *Knowledge Management in the Learning Society*. Paris: The Organization for Economic Cooperation and Development (OECD).

OECD (2006). *Live Longer Work Longer*. Paris: The Organization for Economic Cooperation and Development (OECD).

Rainbird, H., Fuller, A., and Munro, A. (Eds.). (2004). *Workplace Learning in Context*. Abingdon, Oxon: Routledge.

Rasmussen, D., and Swindal, J. (Eds.). (2002). *Habermas-The Foundations of Habermas's Project* (Vol. 1). London: Sage.

Redecker, C., Leis, M., Leendertse, M., Punie, Y., Gijsbers, G., Kirschner, P., Stoyanov, S., and Hoogveld, B. (2011). *The Future of Learning: Preparing for Change*. European Commission Joint Research Centre Institute for Prospective Technological Studies, EUR 24960 EN. Luxembourg: Publications Office of the European Union. http://ipts.jrc.ec.europa.eu/publications/pub.cfm?id=4719 [Accessed 27/3/2017].

Ritzer, G. (2012). *Sociological Theory* (8th edn.). New York: McGraw Hill.

Rogers, C. (1969). *Freedom to Learn: A View of What Education Might Become*. Columbus, OH: Merrill.

Rogers, C. (1983). *Freedom to Learn for the 80s*. New York: Merrill Wright.

Rogers, C., and Freiberg, H.J. (1993). *Freedom to Learn* (3rd edn.). New York: Merrill Wright.

Schmidt, K. (2010). 'Barriers to and Benefits of Further Vocational Training for Older Employees'. In The European Centre for the Development of Vocational Training, Cedefop (Eds.), *Working and Ageing-Emerging Theories and Empirical Perspectives*. Luxembourg: Publications of the European Union.

Schuller, T., and Watson, D. (2009). *Learning Through Life-Inquiry into the Future for Lifelong Learning*. Leicester: National Institute of Adult Continuing Education (NIACE).

Sen, A. (1992). *Inequality Reexamined*. Oxford: Clarendon Press.

Sen, A. (1993). 'Capability and Well-being'. In M. Nussbaum and A. Sen (Eds.), *The Quality of Life*. Oxford: Clarendon Press.

Skolverket. (2000). *Lifelong Learning and Lifewide Learning*. Report for Swedish National Agency for Education. Stockholm: Liber Distribution.

Slee, R. (2010). *The Irregular School*. London, Abingdon, Oxon: Routledge.

SSDA (Sector Skills Development Agency) (2007). *Training, Job Satisfaction and Establishment Performance*. Research Report 22. Wath-upon-Dearne: SSDA. http://dera.ioe.ac.uk/8076/1/070531-r-research-report-22.pdf [Accessed 5/5/2018].

Sutherland, J. (1998). *Workplace Learning for the Twenty-First Century*. Report of the Workplace Learning Task Group. London: Unison.

Terry, P.R. (1997). 'Habermas and education: knowledge, communication, discourse'. *Curriculum Studies*, *5(3)*, 269–279.

Tikkanen, T., and Nyhan, B. (Eds.). (2006). *Promoting Lifelong Learning for Older Workers: An International Overview*. Cedefop Reference series 65. The European Centre for the Development of Vocational Training. Luxembourg: Office for Official Publications of the European Communities. www.cedefop.europa.eu/EN/publications/13019.aspx [Accessed 15/4/2018].

UNESCO (1972). *Learning to be Report – The World of Education Today and Tomorrow*. http://unesdoc.unesco.org/images/0000/000018/001801e.pdf [Accessed 5/10/2018].

UNESCO (2015). *Rethinking Education*. https://en.unesco.org/node/270739 [Accessed 8/8/2018].

Unwin, L. (2009). *Connecting Workplace Learning and VET to Lifelong Learning, Beyond Current Horizons*. http://citeseerx.ist.psu.edu/viewdoc/download?doi=10.1.1.595.3271&rep=rep1&type=pdf [Accessed 24/10/2016].

Unwin, L., Davey, G., Fuller, A., and Leonard, P. (2015). *Supporting an Ageing Workforce: Implications for Working Life, Training and Skills Policy in England. A Literature Review*. Centre for Learning and Life Chances in Knowledge Economies and Societies (LLAKES). www.llakes.ac.uk [Accessed 24/10/2016].

Unwin, L., Felstead, A., Fuller, A., Bishop, D., Lee, T., Jewson, N., and Butler, P. (2007). 'Looking inside the Russian doll: the interconnections between context, learning and pedagogy in the workplace'. *Pedagogy, Culture & Society*, *15(3)*, 333–348.

Vroom, V.H. (1964). *Work and Motivation*. London: Wiley & Sons.

Vygotsky, L. (1978). 'Interaction between Learning and Development'. In M. Cole, V. John-Steiner, S. Scribner, & E. Souberman (Eds.), *Mind and Society: The Development of Higher Psychological Processes*, 79–91. Cambridge, MA: Harvard University Press.

Wenger, E. (1998). *Communities of Practice: Learning, Meaning, and Identity*. Cambridge: Cambridge University Press.

3 Learning in a higher education workplace

This chapter, Part 1 of two related chapters (Chapter 4 being Part 2), explores research conducted in one UK-based higher education (HE) setting focused on those in a wide range of professional and administrative roles and centred on older workers' development and learning.

The conducted research offers the potential for a theory of integration of older workers' learning shown later in Chapter 7. Qualitative data was collected in a two-phase setting, from an institution wide survey, self-selected for those aged 50+ and through interviews with older staff aged 50+ (with no age limit). Senior management, holding roles in strategic human resourcing and development were interviewed. Part 2, which follows in Chapter 4, focuses on organisational considerations for learning and development for older workers based on the study's findings. Here, further themes arising from the research are discussed alongside relevant literature leading to a model and a theory of integration of learning needs which revises the earlier conceptual framework to reframe and re-imagine later life learning for older workers and which is presented in Chapter 7, alongside the concepts and key ideas that emerged from the findings, using the notion of transitions as a baseline for renewal and development.

The key findings of the HE study are now presented under major themes connected to organisational context and processes. Verbatim staff and management participant quotes assigned to older workers are given as (OW) and for management as (M).

Overall, the research uncovered a requirement for spaces for dialogue, the valuing of older workers, informal learning, validating experience, lack of support for age blind professional development, lack of mobility/career progression (despite an eagerness to continue in careers) and that older workers' development required an alignment to strategic HRM planning. The interview findings indicated that themes of equality and diversity, organisational policy, value and perceptions, vulnerability, lack of understanding around transitions and mobility, knowledge sharing, intergenerational dialogue and professional development approaches were important. The research phases were contrasted with external documentation. Internal documentation, representing official dialogue with management, was analysed and cross-referenced against findings including references to the UK Equality Act PSED (2010) in eliminating discrimination, advancing equality of opportunity and fostering good relations between persons who share relevant protected characteristics and those who do not.

Part 1 organisational considerations for the older workforce – context and processes

Organisational models and planning for learning and development

All management in the study recognised the value of development and that it was incumbent upon the organisation to fund development as the university's strategic staff development plan set out. However, development was focused on roles and fixed on organisational benefits, not invested for those to move on. Who funded professional staff development over and above fee remission for formal academic qualifications was not transparent with no central policy.

Management recognised that the UK's default retirement age (DRA) posed challenges for succession planning. Flexible working policies for older workers, implementation of procedures and policies would be required. The benefits of having older workers' contributions reviewed drew on wider evidence from those baby boomers still working and in their influence on government. Benefits should be reviewed due to changing demographics and how an organisation used older workers' skills was commented on by a senior manager.

> So that is one of the things I do welcome about the DRA, that we're no longer seeing them as ready for the scrap heap just because ... But it's about how the organisation utilises their skills that is the key and how we get others to see the benefits.
>
> (M)

For this organisation the approach to career development and to promotion was age blind with no segregation for any aspect. The benefits too of having older workers would need to be reviewed. An evolving intelligent view of older workers' contribution to the workplace and how the organisation used older workers' skills would be necessary. Furthermore, how to get others to see those same benefits was also required. Organisational policies for older workers would need revision of procedures and policies and their implementation.

Equality and diversity for development

In this case study, management considered there was a positive organisational view about diverse workforces with a positive image around age in relation to older workers compared to other organisations, although it was not clear how the benchmarking was arrived at. The workforce demographics data indicated an ageing population. "Some people are around the age of late 70s . . . which we felt was a real positive for the organisation" (M). However, the case of age is slightly different because by and large the distribution of authority in the organisation is run by older people. "So, it works very differently, much more insidious and difficult to deal with" (M).

Whether the hierarchical nature hindered development was contested as the organisation was supposed "to be pushing equity and diversity" but contrastingly it stifled moving on. A further aspect of diversity and equity revolved around what is equitable access to development opportunities, when for instance, caring responsibilities for elderly parents catapulted this issue into an equity concern around equitable access to professional development. Any government policy needs to consider that such access cuts across both legal and human rights principles.

There was a majority view by senior management that the professional development of older workers was not taken seriously. However, one commented that development was probably not taken seriously for anybody "I don't think we take the development of older workers less seriously than anybody else." Nonetheless, being nondiscriminatory was strongly emphasised:

> As Chief Executive, if I came across someone who took the view that we shouldn't develop X because he [sic] is too old I would go through the roof.
>
> (M)

Retention was not a priority, it being informally accepted people would move on in academic and professional life with little done to retain them, attested by both survey and interview data.

Spaces for dialogue appear very important in ensuring inclusion and equal opportunities, aligned to Habermas' notions of dialogic spaces (1987).

Discrimination and value

The word "*discrimination*", although not much evidenced related to age, was raised in relation to general questions of equity such as men promoted over women for doing less work (OW). If discrimination existed in different manifestations one staff member said "I'm not aware of it but it happens everywhere else, why would this organisation be different? It does with men and older support staff, that's what society suggests."

Discriminatory attitudes were felt to be an issue at all levels not just for support staff but took the shape of low levels of discrimination, such as churlishness and disdain showed to an older worker. But the picture was inconsistent, "it might be women generally. I think that it is an issue at all levels, not just support staff" (OW).

There was a concern whether older workers' opportunities were being shut down due to focusing on "young blood" or "whether management was still supporting older workers' careers" (OW). Management made no reference to this form of workplace inclusivity apart from indicating a positive profile of older workers. With age a protected characteristic in the same way as gender, race and ethnicity the interviews probed:

INTERVIEWER: *What I'm trying to uncover: is it perceived differently because it is age, has it had as much attention paid to it as other characteristics?*

> Not from a strategic point of view but one of the things I'm aware of and have tried to encourage is the way in which we use colleagues, for example, Emeritus professors and others to help those coming up the ranks so to speak. I do think more communication needs to be had about how we are able to support . . . we talk about age, the younger ones . . . and still at the same time, support, enthuse, motivate the more senior workers and have the communication, we might get them talking about how one could support the other.
>
> (M)

One management response was "we're all going to get old but not necessarily changing our sexuality and probably don't find it difficult to change our ethnicity identity, so it is different and needs handling in a different way" (M). But formalised organisational structures were not initially considered helpful. "We don't have an age equality group. Should we? And in the case of the race equality group and the LGBT group, those are very much bottom up" (M).

Specific provision in development for older workers stimulated varied comments from management and staff. Some saw it as irrelevant, discriminatory or as labelling aligned to the survey findings. The university "didn't offer development in terms of stages in life which might be helpful."

But one senior manager expressed difficulties in understanding the requirement for any specific provision:

> To a certain extent age doesn't come into it. So, I'm struggling with the concept other than preretirement and getting ready for not being in work.
>
> (M)

The organisation considered that it offered equitable opportunities looking "at skill sets, particularly through appraisal where people's gaps are and where the organisational needs are, but we're also talking about people's ambition" (M).

However, by not discriminating there may have been inadvertent discrimination shown:

> So, we do not discriminate on the basis of age. It is entirely possible as a direct consequence of that there is an inadvertent ... an *inadvertent discrimination* against older workers, who might themselves think there are some things that are not appropriate for them because they haven't got many years left. I don't think the organisation does have that point of view but by virtue of not having made specific provision it might be a consequence of where we are. And so, I think there is work to be done.
>
> (M)

Mobility and career pathways aligned to diversity and equality

Organisationally, there was a lack of transparency and inequality for mobility related to roles. Pathways for development were not transparent. There was little understanding about who shared the vision for learning in the organisation and the strategy was not coherent. Some management did not see clear career pathways for professional staff; the emphasis being focused on academic staff development and growing stars, a well-trodden policy in academic institutions. Other management viewed policy focused on organisational benefits and did not invest for those to move on.

There was doubt over the organisation's intent to develop staff for another organisation's benefit. Ideas around intention to develop varied, with some managers thinking people should not stagnate and who encouraged moving on and in giving different opportunities. Nevertheless, career progression was by no means homogenous with some older workers winding down, others not necessarily wanting the next grade up, but wanting to deepen skills in the same area and to share their learning and expertise. Having skills for consultancy was proposed, such as skills for self-employment.

Management emphasised diversity and equality in career progression for different ways of working across the professional workforce. Whether working full or part time performance and development still mattered. However, even if it is an organisational principle there was still inadvertent discrimination:

> I don't think I see explicit discrimination. But I think there is probably historic inbuilt discrimination. I guess it (development) is more mechanical ... returning to work after maternity schemes.
>
> (M)

Management affirmed there is career development for the BME grouping but that it had not occurred to management to consider provision for older ages. Career-related training, workshops and an external career service were offered but access to a career or development service was considered helpful by management but no specific mobility or career development for older workers existed. "There is something for BME's, but I don't think they've even thought what shall we do about older workers and is there something for them?"

Of note, older workers perceived themselves to be *viewed by others* as career irrelevant but contrastingly they had a keenness and eagerness to continue their careers. A more holistic view of career trajectories through staff development would be helpful.

Midlife reviews for ageist job markets

Mid-working life reviews suggested by NIACE (2015) were widely welcomed and considered helpful for long-term planning and an in-house career offer was viewed as supportive. Most staff felt they had a joint responsibility to develop careers with individual motivation a driver "my own personal drive and seeing there were opportunities I could take up." But equally it was accepted that it was possible to sit back and do nothing. Senior staff tended to stay, with career mobility considered risky. It was more about the day job but skilling up if someone wanted to take flexible retirement or work as a consultant, such as for self-employment.

With the job market largely presented as ageist, career development becomes more urgent as you age and people over the age of 50 struggle to find employment (McNair 2011). Having firm support for midlife career reviews and establishing links with the career service was welcomed in the staff reviews. Career development will vary so undertaking an assessment of what skills and knowledge provision is required. It was considered that lack of profession specific training opportunities hindered movement into other roles.

Staff retention

Management participants remarked on the paucity of opportunities for mobility internally, career mobility, or career development for older workers, but there was not necessarily a correlation between extensive development and moving up the hierarchy. So, people tended to leave taking skills with them.

More widely, the value of older workers within the organisation and wider society was questioned and a sense of discrimination existed in this workplace among staff participating in the research, particularly felt by female older workers. The extent to which the organisation valued staff was important in encouraging someone with their career, acknowledging not everyone wanted to move. Suggestions included work shadowing opportunities and some level of coaching opportunity. But doubt was expressed about the organisation's intent to develop staff for another organisation's benefit. Mobility could be advantageous if talents were underutilised. Needs assessment and job shadowing could support mobility. This would also be a signal that the organisation valued staff and would encourage retention.

The value between generations was problematic for diversity for some in the study and could push older workers out of the workplace. Presumptions that younger people would have respect for experience and age had largely disappeared. Low-level ageism in disdain shown to older workers (some revolved around comments concerning technology) related to inclusive organisational cultures aligned to evidence, suggesting a development orientation and a supportive development climate promoted retention, as emphasised by Maurer (2002) and Armstrong-Stassen and Schlosser (2007). Nevertheless, experience does not necessarily equate to value, the very experience could inhibit the learning. What was important was the quality of the experience regardless of age.

Transitions – re-imagining and normalising learning for the workforce through phases and transitions

A transition is defined as "the process or a period of changing from one state or condition to another" (Oxford Living Dictionaries 2017). Managing transitions was considered undertaken "reasonably well" with time off and support given for age transitioning. In these findings, organisation consistency needed improvement as line management currently relied on their using good judgement or experience. It was expressed that considerable efforts were made by management to offer a flexible range of development opportunities recognising where people's careers and needs might be, but there was much more to do at transition points.

Several staff considered there was an absence of valuing in a *sense of closing down* suggesting *a kind of limbo* for older workers with the organisation not seeing the benefits and "how you move forward than seeing it as the end of your career" and "neither supported to retire and no conversations about benefits of having older workers. Whereas, it should be around valuing and respecting and saying, 'yes, we need you . . . what can I do to help you?'" There was a blurring of spaces between individual personal life and workplace life, seen widely in contemporary workplaces. Staff emphasised elderly caring responsibilities as a growing phenomenon but there exists a sense of burdening in asking for time off.

INTERVIEWER: *Because it's going to impact more in the workplace?*

> Discussion fora or groups where people could openly discuss those issues would be really helpful and because you would know other people were in the same situation. And, you don't feel "God, I've got to phone up and say I need another day off . . . elderly relatives have had another fall or whatever."
>
> (OW)

Organisational consistency needed improvement as line management currently relies on an individual manager's experience and initiative.

Drawing on research into adult development, Bridges (1980) considers the often difficult process of letting go of an old situation, suffering the confusion of being in inbetween states and launching forth again in a new situation. In this way, transitions can be viewed as a theory of personal development, where the natural process of disorientation and reorientation marks the turning points of the path of growth (ibid:5). and ultimately self-renewal. Such a viewpoint can act as a lever in reframing and re-imagining older workplaces, but also in moving beyond one specific workplace as Dewey suggests (Dewey 1995). This means that an older worker can view themselves in a permanent state of self-development which has no externally socially constructed cutoff point. As Bridges with Bridges (1980) points out, many have invested so long in seeing little of value to be gained in transitions that it is difficult to embark on the period of nothingness that proceeds the beginning of renewal. Kubler-Ross (1969) in discussing the five stages of grief suggests that we move from denial to anger, to bargaining, to depression and finally to acceptance. When applied to transitioning in the workplace this suggests that considered development and training could support the process.

Transitions are as much about endings as they are about new starts. In the workplace, these endings and new starts could be in not achieving a longed-for promotion, a move to flexible working or in reducing hours to working part-time. It needs to be recognised that transitions are stressful, physically, emotionally and socially. Each individual will have his or her own response to change.

Intergenerational dialogue, knowledge sharing and team working

Facilitating communication between different age groups and different stages to discuss age hadn't really been considered. Whether intergenerational spaces should be created where people could share tacit knowledge was mixed. Staff interaction with younger age groups would be helpful "touching on that experience thing." Neither management nor staff thought formalised approaches existed, but it was thought by some to happen naturally through ordinary team and staff meetings and good heads of department would facilitate it, although there was a question mark over the wisdom of its institutionalisation.

Healthy working relationships, having validation around experience based on respect where people needed to feel *equally valued* regardless of generation, was important. It could improve business effectiveness using those with vast experience in their working careers which they can share, the good and the bad, "whereas somebody just starting out – what you really want to avoid is reinventing the wheel, you know" (OW). But compositions of future work-places should avoid "*the curse of the gerontocracy*" in having too many older workers, as well as too few. (OW).

There was almost unanimous enthusiasm that informal knowledge sharing was positive and should be further encouraged. Older workers had much they can help young workers with in terms of experience and wealth of knowledge to bring to knowledge sharing. Knowledge exchange was valued as a mechanism for keeping that person engaged in a different way as they move towards the last 5–10 years or whatever of working careers. There didn't appear to be any kind of formal/informal mechanisms for cascading knowledge, it was left to individual initiative. How knowledge was shared and proliferated, set around professional advancement was poorly addressed. But doubt as to whether to institutionalise it was raised, aligned to findings on intergenerational sharing and the value it brings.

But knowledge sharing provoked sensitivity about to whom sharing was of value to:

> There's an informal exchange process of knowledge sharing but unless there is something specific for you as an individual, it might be very useful for the organisation or the department but it's not going to happen.
>
> (OW)

Sharing knowledge was affected by a wider industry climate and power issues where "people fight hard to protect what they know and the area they know" and was acknowledged by management. This view is not limited to higher education workplaces. Some departments appeared more advanced than others with people supporting each other, learning from other members of staff "feeding back knowledge from central programmes at team meetings and individuals being motivated to ask questions and help each other in team work." It was thought that "formalised sessions could be run – very explicit for different perspectives" and more done to get "dialogue going to hear about experiences but carefully couched."

Valuing older workers

Armstrong-Stassen (2008), suggests that the extent to which an organisational culture was valuing older workers is important in that older workers' well-being can affect their motivation to learn. In this study, an ambivalent attitude in the internal culture was reinforcing a sense of older workers *viewing themselves* as career irrelevant. This sense of confinement and limitation was further heightened in that an individual's career was viewed as more narrowly focused on development for the utility of the organisation. Also, though a third in the study considered there was mutual benefit to the organisation and workers from professional development, a significant quarter held no opinion. More generally, it was considered harder for women to be taken as seriously as men.

Perceptions and labelling and its effect on the workplace

A change of perception was needed "rather than us being a burden I think we should be more of an experience" (OW). Several recognised traditional hierarchies, where older people were respected by younger people, have disappeared in workplaces and society meaning "younger people think older people have nothing to teach them – they're *retreads*." One interviewee questioned the value between the generations "it's very important for them to understand where you're coming from and you're not just *old fodder or the dinosaur left behind*." A solution was to "formalise spaces for dialogue to shake up preconceptions people have about each other, where young and old are both present."

Perception is linked to labelling. Some interviewees saw "experience related" as positive and acceptable, a euphemism, one of labelling, did not like either term, had no strong feelings, not needed and those who viewed "age-related" as ageist. For some, the difficulty was not so much the kind of language used but expectations of what you do when older. Labelling can arrest development as "people get assigned as being X and it's very difficult for them to break out of whatever they've been assigned or perceived or not" (OW). Words like "retirement" and "older workers" carried baggage and "experience related" implied experience is valued, when often with older workers, it is the experience which actually gets in the way of the learning said one team leader; "it's the quality of the experience regardless of their age."

Agentic workers

Older workers had a role to play in closing the gap. Staff perceived a default rhetoric around older people with widespread negative views of being a societal burden suggested by Tikkanen and Nyhan (2006). Significantly, and representing a disjunct with the organisation and society more widely, the older workers in this study realised they were not passive recipients; they had a role to play and furthermore should make efforts to close the gap. This action orientated view is supported by critical educational gerontology (Findsen and Formosa 2011:54), being a positive approach to "helping people better understand and assist themselves." It is concerned with political structures and powers underpinning learning and the role of older people themselves to shape the social system in which it is established, reflecting a Foucauldian perspective (Foucault 1977).

Having work agency, proposed by Harteis and Goller (2014), was a powerful mechanism to get what was needed in staff development. Fostering a good relationship with the staff development unit was pivotal in this study. Having an approachable head of staff development signalled the importance of an enabling leadership style and culture in encouraging participation aligned to Bass and Avolio's work (1994). Being proactive in contributing suggestions for development courses suggests the aspect of the emphasis on self-efficacy as advanced by Maurer et al. (2003). Putting staff in control supported them to be proactive. In turn, building work agency, proposed by Harteis and Goller (2014), giving capacity to interact within a community of practice as emphasised by Cairns and Malloch (2010) was supportive in extending learning.

Vulnerability: the horror of ageing. Understanding how age impacts on perception, feelings and confidence and the language around older workers

Management recognised older workers could experience vulnerability in ageing:

> I suspect they do, ageing is terrible really. It's horrible. Again, if there is evidence the organisation through its processes, practices or policies is doing things that is making people feel vulnerable, I would like to know what they are.
>
> (M)

Female older workers were particularly affected:

> In the administration, the majority of staff are female; a good proportion of female older workers ... I think they feel vulnerable and lack confidence. They don't have parity of esteem and are at the lower grades.
>
> (M)

One manager thought many would be afraid of being denied development if the organisation knew they might exit in five years and the approach should be to help those transition. Many staff reported vulnerability around age, losing their jobs, status, potency, health and in professional life. "Probably the most important single factor is not to destroy their confidence." How older workers are perceived goes very much into society when hearing about people in their fifties plus being made redundant finding it very hard to get jobs, as research indicates (McNair 2011).

Those viewing the term "having experience" as positive and acceptable, and those viewing it as negative, raised a point about workplace terminology; whether it acted as a progression or a barrier in people's minds in line with the former trade union the National Association of Teachers in Further and Higher Education (NATFHE) (2016) proposition (now part of the University and College Union [UCU]). Retirement was viewed as pejorative. Being in that phase was not the issue but connotations and expectations of what you do when you are older were. Labelling stops or arrests the ability to break out of what participants had been assigned to or perceived to be, resulting in discrimination of older workers. Such language created an atmosphere where it was possible to bully people into unwanted premature retirement. A language of equality, such as speaking of "long-serving" colleagues rather than the "middle aged" or "old guard," may help avoid some unwanted intimidation (ibid.). Relating "experience" to professional development, language could be used positively thereby encouraging participation to attract those reluctant to engage. Individually, older workers should take responsibility by "avoiding self-labelling and engaging in self-prophecy related to perceived limitations" and create and participate in learning opportunities as advanced by Findsen (2015:587).

Empowerment and improving confidence was a very significant finding, where learning is pivotal. An IES/NIACE study (Hillage et al. 2000) indicated that there was improved confidence and willingness to shoulder responsibility through learning experiences.

Holistic aspects of well-being related to learning

In this HE study, an overwhelming majority wanted a better work–life balance and a third desired to work flexibly borne out by the Altmann Report (2014), and the Foresight Report (2008).

Health aspects "which absolutely would have implications for organisations" were raised. With older workers staying on a further decade or more, staff will experience significant illnesses. Health vulnerability refers to both older men and women, while female health issues such as menopause and its implications were rarely considered. Female older workers were particularly susceptible in other areas due to taking on caring roles.

Chapter 4 as Part 2 focuses on organisational considerations for learning and development for older workers based on the key findings for this same HE study.

References

Altmann, R. (2014). *A New Vision for Older Workers: Retain, Retrain and Recruit.* London: Department for Work and Pensions.

Armstrong-Stassen, M. (2008). 'Factors associated with job content plateauing among older workers'. *Career Development International, 13(7)*, 594–613.

Armstrong-Stassen, M., and Schlosser, F. (2007). 'Benefits of a supportive development climate for older workers'. *Journal of Managerial Psychology, 23(4)*, 419–437.

Bass, B.M., and Avolio, B.J. (1994). 'Transformational leadership and organizational culture'. *International Journal of Public Administration, 17(1)*, 112–121.

Bridges, W., with Bridges, S. (1980). *Managing Transitions: Making the Most of Change.* London: Nicholas Brealey Publishing.

Cairns, L., and Malloch, M. (2010). 'Theories of Work, Place and Learning: New Directions'. In M.Malloch, L. Cairns, K. Evans and B. O'Connor (Eds), *The Sage Handbook of Workplace Learning.* London: Sage.

Dewey, J. (1995). 'Education as Growth'. In R.B. Goodman (Ed.), *Pragmatism: A Contemporary Reader.* Abingdon-on-Thames: Routledge.

Findsen, B. (2015). 'Older workers' learning within organisations: issues and challenges'. *Educational Gerontology, 41(8)*, 582–589.

Findsen, B., and Formosa, M. (2011). *Lifelong Learning in Later life: A Handbook on Older Adult Learning.* Rotterdam: Sense.

Foresight Mental Capital and Wellbeing Project (2008). *Final Project Report.* London: The Government Office for Science.

Foucault, M. (1977). *Discipline and Punish: The Birth of the Prison.* Trans. Alan Sheridan. New York: Pantheon.

Government Equalities Office (2011). *Equality act 2010: Public Sector Equality Duty, What Do I Need to Know? A Quick Start Guide for Public Sector Organisations, Government Equalities Office.* https://ucu.custhelp.com/ci/fattach/get/48448/1304941461/redirect/1/filename/General%20Equality%20Duty%20Guide%20April%202011.pdf [Accessed 15/6/2018].

Habermas, J. (1987). *The Theory of Communicative Action* (Vol. 2). Trans. T. McCarthy. Cambridge: Polity Press.

Harteis, C., and Goller, M. (2014). 'New Skills for New Jobs: Work Agency as a Necessary Condition for Successful Lifelong Learning'. In T. Halttunen, M. Koivisto and S. Billett (Eds.), *Promoting, Assessing, Recognizing and Certifying Lifelong Learning – International Perspectives and Practices.* Dordrecht: Springer.

Hillage, J., Uden, T., Aldridge, F., and Eccles, J. (2000). *Adult Learning in England: A Review.* Leicester: Institute for Employment Studies (IES) and National Institute of Adult Continuing Studies (NIACE).

Kubler-Ross, E. (1969). *On Death and Dying.* New York: Macmillan.

Maurer, T.J. (2002). 'Employee learning and development orientation. Toward an integrative model of involvement in continuous learning'. *Human Resource Development Review, 1(1)*, 9–44.

Maurer, T.J., Wrenn, K.A., Pierce, H.R., Tross, S.A., and Collins, W.C. (2003). 'Beliefs about improvability of career-relevant skills: relevance to job/task analysis, competency modelling and learning orientation'. *Journal of Organizational Behavior, 24(1)*, 107–131.

McNair, S. (2011). *Older People and Skills in a Changing Economy.* London: UK Commission for Employment and Skills.

National Association of Teachers in Further and Higher Education (NATFHE) (2016). A NATFHE Guide to Equality Language. https://www.ucu.org.uk/article/1865/Site-search?q=a+guide+to+equality+language.

NIACE (2015). *Extending Working Life through Career Review at Mid-life.* Leicester: NIACE.

Oxford Living Dictionaries (2017) https://en.oxforddictionaries.com/definition/transition.

Tikkanen, T., and Nyhan, B. (Eds.). (2006). *Promoting Lifelong Learning for Older Workers: An International Overview.* Cedefop Reference series 65. The European Centre for the Development of Vocational Training. Luxembourg: Office for Official Publications of the European Communities. www.cedefop.europa.eu/EN/publications/13019.aspx [Accessed 15/4/2018].

4 Organisational considerations

As Part 2, following on from Chapter 3, this chapter focuses on organisational considerations for learning and development. The role of dialogue in exploring holistic learning and development for the older worker is explored. The types and forms of professional development and workplace learning that would offer a best fit based on the research into a higher education workplace which will also have implications for other organisations are reviewed.

10.0 learning and development – dialogue, forms and review

Establishing dialogue between management and staff to identify age-related professional development had not been considered apart from preretirement courses. However, management concurred that staff review and development, one-to-ones, focus groups on issues and staff training development analysis in the annual staff questionnaire would provide a channel for dialogue.

Notably, staff in this research widely recognised there was insufficient dialogue around development. Examples of having spaces for voices to be heard included management being visible around departments, having good role models and facilitation of situations where people felt comfortable opening up. Mechanisms included discussion groups, fora to ascertain age-related needs, focus groups, role models, tools for reflection on future options and cross fertilisation of ideas. Suggestions from staff also included using the staff review and development process and a strategic lead from senior leadership. Dialogue was needed between line managers of older workers and staff development but the role of individuals in development was also critical, but which needed sensitive handling. In this particular context, development took place within departments and teams, involving staff development and where team priorities were supported.

Development needed to be more "alive" and dynamic which would also minimize isolation in the workplace, aligned to Kanfer and Ackerman's research (2004) which indicates that knowledge utilisation, helping, collaboration and enhancing positive affect seen as motivators were not addressed in either theory or practice at this site, which could improve participation in development.

Communication and understanding can provide a mechanism for valuing what older workers offer. However, the findings suggested different groups at different stages in the university did not come together as a norm, so formalised spaces for dialogue through creating "Habermasian spaces" called for by Barnett (2012), could break up preconceptions and empower. This aspect will become increasingly important in the future as staff work remotely using technology and increasingly work flexibly, therefore opportunities to come together will be inconsistent and less frequent and without spaces for dialogue the Habermasian ideal will be limited.

Significantly, consultation by staff with management on formal committees which had staff development on their agenda to permit voices to be heard was not raised. Neither was consultation with staff development mentioned apart from acknowledging emails were circulated and the staff review form canvassed further suggestions. This again was significant given consultative committees had staff development on the agenda.

Dialogue with trade unions is also crucial. Nurturing positive collaborative relations with trade unions is important as underscored by Duncan (2014). In this study, documentary findings showed trade union perceptions were included in decision-making for HR development but importantly, and most curiously, neither management nor staff participants mentioned the role of the recognised unions in discussing age-related concerns, despite unions holding frequent meetings for members onsite where concerns for increased dialogue could be raised. Oosterwikj's (2015) research considers that trade unions have been coy around advocating for older workers' retention, so unions could and should play an increased role.

Maintaining currency as an older worker

Management and staff both valued maintaining currency "particularly for an organisation having a strong professional development and education focus" with opportunities given in skilling or moving sideways, or because things are developing generally, e.g. technology. Older workers must have the confidence through training and discussion "to speak up when things blocking them could be related to other people's perceptions of them as old." Perceptions needed to shift to acknowledge development, "we're all encouraged to work so we need to continue to be motivated and supported. You don't want to apologise because you're 60 and you want to continue your career". There may be gaps in perception, with assumptions made about appropriate development needs concentrated on "maintenance rather than progression when an older worker may actually want to be creating new pathways and new engagement".

However, most striking and concerning in today's fast changing world was that only half of the participants in this study held any opinion on gaps in development, indicating a significant staleness and a certain lack of ambition in reflecting on goals and where refreshment is required. This finding emphasised an urgency to reflect on development approaches in the second half of life to protect against both unemployment and remain employable, particularly when the findings indicated a lack of impetus in thinking about developmental goals in line with McNair (2006) and Altmann's (2014) research.

Forms of professional development best matching the needs of older workers and transitions

In the research, staff considered that age-blind Professional Development (PD) should be needs related regardless of career path, wide-ranging and open to all ages. Differentiation was largely considered inappropriate. Over half the participants were uninterested in age-related development. Segregated professional development for older workers was either viewed as irrelevant, discriminatory, labelling or development that was segregated in terms of life stages and transitions was viewed as being unhelpful. Nevertheless, as mentioned in Chapter 2, career development applied to everyone becomes more urgent as you age in an ageist job market, with those aged 50+ struggling to be employed as McNair (2009, 2011) suggests.

Views over whether development provision should be age-related or tailored were polarised with as many for as against which may represent a fear of being seen as old. However, tailored provision keeps older workers employable (McNair 2006; Altmann 2014). Having an emphasis on mid-working life reviews suggested by NIACE (2015) were very valued in this workplace.

Interestingly, management stated staff had not specifically asked for any age-related development or referred to it in an age-related way, so it had never been looked at in that sense. Organisational development programmes had concentrated on equitable development opportunities for all, preferring to view people as individuals addressing their individual, professional and personal needs, skills sets and aspirations. The only exception was preretirement planning. Although management saw it as not discriminating on the basis of age, a key finding was that it was acknowledged by senior management that as a direct consequence of not making specific provision for older workers (who might think they did not have many years of work left) an inadvertent discrimination may be taking place.

Nonetheless, management acknowledged staff required development at different ages and career stages. But the organisation needed more investment in development to keep the workforce current and renewed as longevity in the workforce can result in loss of skills seen in other research (McNair et al. 2006; McNair 2010, Altmann 2014). So, more reengagement with older workers than younger workers is required in terms of refreshment such as advancement of technology as an AAT (2015) report indicated, which may present some challenges to identity and furthermore raises a suggestion of discriminatory practices. Also, although the organisation appears to be doing a reasonable job of supporting staff to keep up with technology, older workers can find learning new systems and technology challenging (AAT 2015), indicating further support was required.

One manager considered, "it is how you keep them current by investing more in *refresh and reengagement* with older workers than with younger workers, refreshment in what is happening in the world out there. We're all the same." All management interviewed thought a midlife career review was positive as "there is nothing for professional staff."

Transitioning and development

But broader development in transitions was not really recognised "inevitably impacting more on older women than on younger women or men" which raises discriminatory concerns.

Most staff were aware of retiring workshops but didn't consider there was development given apart from "the retirement thing which is about retiring," but there was no provision for different life stages. Management too acknowledged more could be done around preretirement.

> It's not "retirement" anymore ... not sure what the word is, and something could be done in the last 10–12 years of work. A staged withdrawal would help due to increasing workload pressure ... I'm sure I'm not alone in this.
>
> (OW)

Apart from retirement workshops, how to manage later career years was difficult. Possibilities for development exist with retraining, training for alternatives, work opportunities, establishing coaching, shadowing and proactively encouraging movement and mentoring. Other suggestions included refreshers, confidence boosters and reflecting on achievements. There was a lack of homogeneity though and for those nearing retirement age there were difficulties in finding out the issues related to stepping away from the workplace. For some, it is a focus on an exit strategy but for others it is more about coping with changing everyday demands.

Soft skills and experience; team working, empathy skills, negotiation skills of use in intergenerational and knowledge sharing were considered valuable but often went unnoticed. Soft skills were needed but "soft skills people aren't necessarily the ones who are getting promoted" admitted management. Other scenarios for encouraging learning included; management prompts, scenarios to pull everybody in and sharing of different life journeys "to get the message across loud and clear that c'mon we're talking to everybody. So that it's important and valuable to the individual, group, and organisation and we can all benefit." There needs to be a massive range of development for all ages "which is not a one-size-fits-all, it comes back to personalising learning." There was a suggestion to formalise networking learning through professional learning communities "but we are several stages behind that."

Management acknowledged types of development currently offered were not the best fit:

> The sorts that work are by and large not what is provided. It is about mentoring, coaching, workplace relationships, team working, partnerships; it's about the unfunded, uncosted bits of development.
>
> (M)

Both management and staff views emphasised the value of development through coaching, mentoring, relationships and team work reinforced through holistic learning found in communities of practice and coaching and mentoring models as Evans, Waite and Kersh (2010a) advocate. Nonetheless, it was the forms of professional development viewed as most valuable that were uncosted in this university study.

Forging self-identity as an older worker and feeling valued through learning – value and perceptions

Overwhelmingly, management were not considered to be fully supportive of development for older age workers. Only a minority of staff believed that older staff were valued by the organisation. Overall, this perception suggests management may at best be lukewarm and, at worst, not actively supportive of older workers. But there was inconclusive agreement over the extent that organisational culture was seen to value older workers as raised by Armstrong-Stassen (2008), suggesting an ambivalent attitude in the internal culture was reinforcing a sense of older workers viewing themselves as career irrelevant. This sense of confinement and limitation was further heightened in that an individual's career was potentially viewed as more narrowly focused on development for the utility of the organisation. Even though a third considered there was mutual benefit to the organisation and workers from the standpoint of professional development, a significant quarter held no opinion.

Issues around identity were provocative as over 50% of staff wanted their informal learning experiences recognised by other staff and management as a way of representing their value in the workplace. This suggested older workers' knowledge and experience could be underutilised as McNair's (2011) research suggested.

Possessing interpersonal skills was highly valued, related to notions of self-identity, which aligns to the literature (Evans, Guile and Harris 2010b:160). Older workers wanting recognition of the value of their interpersonal skills represents a significant finding, but as indicated earlier, soft skills were not valued by the organisation and did not lead to promotion and career progression. This is an important omission as the value of, and recognition of older workers' informal learning experiences, is overwhelmingly validated in Evans et al. (2004) research. Mentoring, proposed by Evans, Waite and Kersh

(2010a), was highly valued by staff in this research, as were establishing communities of practice, aligned to Cairns and Malloch's (2010) work.

Feeling valued in the workplace is an aspect of diversity, being in line with the CIPD's (2018) argument that being "valued" is critical to the psychological contract employees have with employers. A literature scan around valuing professional managerial and administrative staff in HE reveals a complete paucity of literature as far as I could decipher. However, Duncan (2014) considers that universities are considered largely effective in demonstrating they value staff through the existence of surveys, follow-up action plans, reports, fora and working groups where staff can participate.

Making work more attractive to older workers to encourage participation and workplace retention

Making work more attractive to older workers encourages retention and professional development mirroring key processes which broadens understanding of workplace learning for 21st-century challenges and how we learn in a variety of places. These processes emphasise tacit learning, that is, elements of mastery drawing on everyday practice which are beneficial in sustaining adult learning as Evans, Kersh and Kontiainen's findings indicate (2004). This was crucial when the organisation's adoption of adult learning pedagogies was not always present and importantly such processes encourage older workers' engagement aligned to the literature (Evans and Kersh 2004).

A broader conception of what development is would help participation and make it more relevant, an everyday occurrence, applicable to both staff and management. This could include "coaching and mentoring" in the formal box but more self-directed knowledge such as meeting with peer colleagues, reading around the subject, writing, participating in national working groups, "to me, that's all development . . . at my stage of career they're the more valuable." Utilising staff development personal development plans, encouraging honesty and trust so information can inform and the organisational support, is considered helpful as is coaching around retirement.

Self-worth through participation in development and the role of line management

Making time for development is important "because it comes back to the question of self-promotion and self-worth. If they don't do it and you've got a line manager who's not doing it, what happens is they're stuck forever unless they leave." Staff and management seemed agreed that to some extent older people became humbler in age, "you feel less confident about lots of things but more confident about others – there's quite a lot of research on this." Management have responded with work experience, peer placement, targeted programmes for women, men and BAME staff and encouragement to take up Erasmus programmes.

The responsibility to push forward/own professional development was thought overall jointly shared but "individuals needed to know they're empowered." Further support was requested as:

> You seem to get stuck at a level and it's very hard to see a way out, progress elsewhere or be given the opportunity, e.g. job shadow, which is not really encouraged, neither is career progression. Whereas, in other organisations it's encouraged and expected.
>
> (OW)

Line managers needed "to adopt specific approaches to understand how age impacts perception, feelings and confidence". Staff development run workshops for line managers focused on equality and diversity, the importance of the staff reviews and development process and the development of those they line managed and for employee engagement. With changing demographics awareness raising for age was needed in future development planning.

Review and development processes and their effectiveness

For this university, the annual staff review and development (SRD) is completed regardless of position or role, academic or professional staff and similarly structured. References to a lack of transparency were commonly heard and where the SRD went once submitted. For one manager, the SRD linked to the overall strategic plan:

> In thinking and making provision in the overall strategic plan for whether we've got the skills and dispositions needed ... so it plays a part in our strategic planning and we direct staff development that they're going to have to do some work.
>
> (M)

But how evidence that learning had an impact on the organisation was gathered, and clarity around how an individual's SRD fed into organisational practice was somewhat surprising:

> Not well, that goes right back to what we were discussing, an individualised, disarticulated culture.

Conversations had been held with staff development about the need to have line of sight between strategic priorities and an individual's objectives. A gap was acknowledged but it was not considered specific to the organisation:

> I think in any institution, the focus tends to be on developing and growing your academic stars and development for professional staff is really discipline based, accountants are going to be trained accountants,

> and I think that is changing ... I think you only get the best out of your professional staff ... there is a business imperative to developing them.
>
> (M)

Generally, staff development was not considered by management as part of integrated strategic planning. "I'm not sure about strategic planning. It will be talked about in the Strategic Plan, around building an inclusive workforce and around leadership skills and developing potential." But for staff, there was a missing organisational link in how the vision translated into staff reviews. For one staff participant, organisational practice is what you do on a day-to-day basis, "so I think it does [feed in] but not formally. It's just about getting the job done really and how we do that." Another viewed the review process as a useful tool for goal setting.

What is clear is that the staff review offered no place for an age-related discussion where dialogue could take place, not exclusively for the older worker, but more around what stage of career that discussion would be helpful to have to open up the dialogue. Management thought there was still a place for learning new skills, e.g. IT, to maintain currency or where through changing technology functions became obsolete.

The SRD form was set up for short-term objectives and did not allow staff to consider different roles, whereas a long-term plan was required. Staff recognised future career progression was just as important as other development. Adopting a broader conception of staff development meant that it would be easier to see how older workers' development could be structured around a busy working life. The SRD could be less structured, "linked into informal learning, learning days, that sort of thing," recognising tacit knowledge. One staff member said that it was helpful having "a personal professional development plan giving people a sense of where they're going and where they want to go. You're being considerably more proactive – it's an individual thing then," suggesting self-agency. A senior manager agreed,

> This would be a reangling of the whole nature of the development portfolio to be able to include this. It's what self-reflected learning is; giving opportunities for open, frank and trusting conversations with a reviewer as to where they are, or with a career service or coach, so colleagues can feel they can have a conversation with someone about 'what next? What else?'

References

AAT (Association of Accounting Technicians) (2015). *The Economic Benefits of Adults Reskilling*. London: Centre for Economics and Business Research Ltd (CEBR).

Altmann, R. (2014). *A New Vision for Older Workers: Retain, Retrain and Recruit*. London: Department for Work and Pensions.

Armstrong-Stassen, M. (2008). 'Factors associated with job content plateauing among older workers'. *Career Development International, 13(7)*, 594–613.

Barnett, R. (2012). *Imagining the University*. London: Routledge.

Cairns, L., and Malloch, M. (2010). 'Theories of Work, Place and Learning: New Directions'. In M. Malloch, L. Cairns, K. Evans and B. O'Connor (Eds.), *The Sage Handbook of Workplace Learning*. London: Sage.

Chartered Institute of Personnel Development (CIPD) (2018). *The Psychological Contract*. Chartered Institute of Personnel Development. www.cipd.co.uk/knowledge/fundamentals/relations/employees/psychological-factsheet#6096 [Accessed 2/9/2018].

Duncan, D. (2014). 'Valuing professional, managerial and administrative staff in HE'. *Perspectives, Policy and Practice in Higher Education, 18(2)*, 38–42.

Evans, K., Waite, E., and Kersh, N. (2010a). 'Towards a Social Ecology of Adult Learning in the Workplace'. In M. Malloch, L. Cairns, K. Evans and B. O'Connor (Eds). *The Sage Handbook of Workplace Learning*. London: Sage.

Evans, K., Guile, D., and Harris, J. (2010b). 'Rethinking Work-Based Learning – For Education Professionals and Professionals Who Educate'. In M. Malloch, L. Cairns, K. Evans and B. O'Connor (Eds.), *The Sage Handbook of Workplace Learning*. London: Sage.

Evans, K., and Kersh, N. (2004). 'Recognition of tacit skills: sustaining learning outcomes in adult learning and work re-entry'. *Journal of Workplace Learning, 16(1/2)*, 63–74.

Evans, K., Kersh, N., and Kontiainen, S. (2004). 'Recognition of tacit skills: sustaining learning outcomes in adult learning and work re-entry'. *International Journal of Training and Development, 8(1)*, 54–72.

Evans, K., Waite, E., and Kersh, N. (2010). 'Towards a Social Ecology of Adult Learning in the Workplace'. In M. Malloch, L. Cairns, K. Evans and B. O'Connor (Eds.), *The Sage Handbook of Workplace Learning*. London: Sage.

Kanfer, R., and Ackerman, P.L. (2004). 'Aging, adult development, and work motivation'. *Academy of Management Review, 29(3)*, 440–458.

McNair, S. (2006). *Older People's Learning – An Action Plan, NIACE*. Leicester. http://www.stephenmcnair.uk/index.php/learning-and-older-people/. [Accessed 1/12/2018]

McNair, S. (2009). *Older People's Learning – An Action Plan*. Leicester: National Institute of Adult Continuing Education (England and Wales).

McNair, S. (2010). *A Sense of a Future - A Study of Training and Work in Later Life*. NIACE. http://shop.niace.org.uk/media/catalog/product/a/_/a_sense_of_a_future_short_report_final_web.pdf [Accessed 18/6/2018].

McNair, S. (2011). *Older People and Skills in a Changing Economy*. London: UK Commission for Employment and Skills.

McNair, S., Flynn, M., and Owen-Hussey, L. (2006). *Older Workers in the South East*. Guildford: Centre for Research into the Older Workforce (CROW).

NIACE (2015). *Extending Working Life through Career Review at Mid-Life – Extending Working Life through Career Review at Mid-Life*. Leicester: NIACE.

Oosterwikj, R.E. (2015). *Policy Frameworks Concerning Older Workers- A Comparative Study of Policy Frameworks and Trade Union Involvement in Sweden and the Netherlands*. Institute of International Education, Stockholm University. Unpublished thesis. http://su.diva-portal.org/smash/get/diva2:818650/FULLTEXT01.pdf [Accessed 24/8/2018].

5 Case studies for learning and development

This chapter explores a variety of perspectives of inclusivity, championing and holistic support for later life learning seen through interviews and case studies providing examples across varying sectors. I am most grateful to those individuals and organisations that have contributed to a broad set of examples and for the permission for their reports and views to be included and published.

BBC – BBC website for England

Laura Ellis, Head of Digital England

BBC Digital England creates a wide range of content, employing 200 people. The Head of Digital England role holds strategic development for editorial and strategic responsibility for England (12 regions) and for those who work for regional TV radio and digital, making up to 6000 staff covering local community, news and sports. I hold a management and leadership role for 50 people and 100 others. The role feeds into central HR and development through working with a range of business partners for HR. There is a safety and contracting and development function as well as development of staff.

Older people are generally more focussed on their career and might be less flexible than they were earlier in their careers. Now, younger people come with video, digital writing skills and audio whereas before they came with radio or TV but no camera capability. For older people, there is often societal bias which says that you can't learn or lift the camera when you are older or be expected to go out at all hours on a job. Partially this is true as when we age we experience issues that potentially limit us.

There are some inevitabilities of life that present further issues. At the BBC, policies are created by our management over childcare, teenage children or ageing parents. This is often called the BLT sandwich generation programme – which covers elderly parents, childcare and household management. It used to be that people worked at a full 100% and then returned but with self-realisation that sometimes it is not possible, and we as management need to understand that. Our department are quite open minded about that. We understand that people have times where they are performing at a different rate, so I want to develop that, so people don't think that is an issue.

Otherwise, there is stress and staff then feel unable to talk to people about it, which often then results in long-term sick leave.

I do have a certain autonomy and I think there is quite a high level of emotional intelligence among BBC managers. We want an environment that takes into consideration family life and where you can discuss and talk with colleagues and bring back collective responsibility for each other. That will get you back into feeling comfortable, so we try and engender that feeling. That is culture. It is the management team that lead that culture. But we need to respect that others too all need and have a right to that care who, for instance, don't have children. We try to prioritise everyone's different needs making sure everyone is afforded that care and attention. This is flexible working offering personal autonomy but within a rota in a news gathering service. However, within that, if managed well, people can have autonomy and feel sufficiently empowered.

In terms of diversity, the BBC is still a bit paternalistic as a vast number of management positions are held by men. In relation to gender pay, the Global Women in News network has been set as a global women's network for those working in news and it covers issues of gender, pay etc. There is an annual BBC survey surveying attitudes to working within the corporation.

There is no steering group on older workers as it has never been thought of. Age at the BBC is interesting. Previously, many staff retired early with an excellent pension which stopped in the late 1990s. Now many are thinking "we're staying on." At 60 people get looked at: "Well, you're be going soon." "When you get to 60 you ought to be thinking about going." I'd like to think a 70-year-old could be working at the BBC – currently it's seen as a novelty and a bit of fun. I'd like to normalise it and not obsess over it.

Culture or practice to address the needs of older people

There is currently no specific culture or practice to address older workers' issues. However, it is an open organisation and the culture permits challenging the bosses. The unions and staff can be very challenging and outspoken, and HR would consider that there should be a focus on older workers if we were to go to them. There is no specific policy or practice around transitions. Going part time is acceptable but there is still an issue around those of 60+. So now there is a conversation that needs to take place. And we should be asking key questions over how we can use the immense experience of the older staff and what it is they would like to do now – currently we don't do that well.

Development for older workers

There is a concern that offering age-related development will feel patronising. It has changed in the last 10 years as people used to be much more flexible around travel. People want to spend more time with families. It was thought there should be development throughout your job. At the BBC, there is recognition that people would want to change departments and a culture of being able to move across departments.

As people age they either feel they can't do something or they go the other way, filled with the confidence that they have the systems, learned from mistakes and can mentor people. Across the BBC, there is reverse mentoring where someone under 30 mentors managers. There is a culture of sharing expertise and support across a wide range of areas. There are both mixed and women leadership development courses. The corporation does not offer a midlife career review, although there is an ad hoc career review and possibility for mobility. There is a very good attachment policy for 2–3 months for a year with a financial allowance. Also, the possibility of a 2-week experiential scheme to try out new areas of work where lots of encouragement to move around is offered.

Diversity policy

The diversity policy encompasses all (except for gender pay). There are specific voices for BAME, younger people and women. But we don't do well with class. If you're working class it is harder to get on.

Older workers don't seem to be an issue as most politicians are older. The BBC generally focuses on portrayal (that is the BBC language for diversity). At present, there is no older network as far as I know. In terms of older females, our Director–General (DG) is an older white-haired man. Some people are saying, "we need a younger DG." However, it doesn't matter what age they are if they can operate the right skills set. There are few older senior females. There is a female Deputy Director General, Anne Bulford and a female Head of HR, Valerie Hughes D'eath. The BBC is keenly awaiting the first woman DG.

How can you make the most of the value of older workers?

We will hit a bump if we don't value our older workers and make it more obvious. I think it is nice to value people bringing in older age and there is some scramble to get rid of people as they are expensive, due to budgetary challenges. Skills people are often anonymous and we need to ask is there a way to record skills and experience and make use of them. We need to make older status more valuable but not go on about pensions. I'd like to see higher status at the BBC for older workers; we don't value their skills and experience in this country.

UK insurance, Aviva

Mary Bright

Mary is External Liaison lead for Andy Briggs, CEO UK Insurance at Aviva and the UK Government's Business Champion for Older Workers. Aviva is working closely with Business in the Community, The Age Campaign.

Our business is about pensions, savings, investments so when looked at it from an analytical point of view with an ageing population, we asked "how do we enable those to have a financially secure old age"? Well, broadly they can work longer, save more, or live in poverty. So, to avoid the last one there needed to be a two-pronged approach to start thinking of financial futures earlier, and secondly, a necessity to continue to be economically active for as long as possible and longer for financial security. If a job is securing a financial future, then with an ageing population we can't ignore the fact that too many of those 50+ are economically inactive and it's the lucky few that can afford to stop work at 50 and enjoy that future. This was at a time when defined pensions were ending and before pension freedoms but we're seeing an increasing number of people that are classifying themselves as retired and probably fuelled by the change in pension freedom.

We looked at that and at attitudinal research to finance alongside age and we realised that people needed help, but also that companies needed to change. Our majority customer base is mainly 50+. So, we spent time thinking what was needed and what help was there to employ people over 50+ and it led us to think about working with The Age Campaign.

From an employer's point of view and looking at the changing overall demographic in UK there is one lens which says that there is no statutory retirement age and age is part of equal opportunities. The other lens is the reducing number of young people entering the jobs market and the decrease in the number of migrants after Brexit occurs. So, to access the widest talent business as a whole, we need to look at the biggest and wider recruitment pool, including age. Quite notable and striking, is the similarity in the research into what millennials want and what research says that people over 50 want. The parallels jump out at you. So, in the areas of work–life balance, work having to have meaning, the ability to continue learning and to share skills comes out in both. The Age Campaign says age is no barrier to work but employers need to be coming from that perspective.

If you take challenges faced by young people, they are told they don't have the right experience for the role or they will face age discrimination. Older workers will also be faced with age discrimination although a different type, but they will face interview scenarios in which they are not necessarily skilled at the beginning, similar to millennials, but it is not due to lack of ability, but the construct established over two generations in what we expect in a traditional work–life trajectory. The Centre for Ageing Better has recent research into what motivates older workers. It found it was what all age groups want, but specifically what millennials want is autonomy, control over work, flexibility and meaning.

If I think about women in workplace, the level of change in their lifetime is possibly unsurpassed since the industrial revolution. So, if you were born a baby boomer it was pre-pill when women stopped work when pregnant or when they married. The norm was to be brought up when the type of work for women was typing pools, teaching and nursing. So, all that gender change that has gone on in parallel to the world of work, that has changed. Then you add in the expectation that women will be economically independent, so when I started work the state pension was 60, mine is now 68. As a young person, I would have expected to have benefitted from a spousal pension after my lifelong partner died, so the very built-in norms that I was brought up with are all false. Everything I learned as a young woman is wrong. Quite a lot of women and men feel they have to "make way for young people." I'm not aware of research on this but it is anecdotal. Men and women both feel it, but I hear it more from women.

We found within Aviva that without any positive intervention those 50+ are 23% less likely to have career discussions with their manager. So, both manager and person/individual were deprioritising in 23% more cases. As a result, we put in an intervention in an organisation where everyone is required to have an annual career conversation but that does require both parties to sit down and make time.

We also did an analysis of performance ratings in comparison to the age of the manager. Our results showed people within the same decade of age as their manager were more likely to be rated at the highest level, regardless of any other factors. If a manager was aged 40 and the person aged 40, then you were rated higher. Regardless of specialism, type of work, area of country – any other variable being like your manager was the strongest determinant.

Unconscious bias has led Aviva to look at unconscious bias training and how we bring age out into that. So much of equality work has focused on gender and race and largely left out or ignored age when society is so youth dominated. So, when you have someone saying "you look good for your age" as a compliment then it is absolutely endemic and comes out not surprisingly absolutely unconsciously. We don't think we have age bias of workers, but we do. And to a greater extent than for gender. And so, it is great that you are doing this research.

The average age of a FTSE company director is 54, so to characterise older workers as all carers and with MS problems is equally countered by those setting up their own business and the numbers of entrepreneurs and those seeking a new career. It's such a huge population, it's impossible to make generalisations and that is why age is no barrier.

The whole concept of lifelong learning is new for a generation who has been used to thinking of one or two jobs or an occupation where you become an expert. Aviva get many speculative CVs from people aged 50+, often from those who have been high up in their field and very well paid and want to transfer but are expecting to be able to transfer at a commensurate salary rate, without retraining. We're still working out how to manage this. If you've had a £50,000 per year job and been economically inactive and then come in as a call handler on £20,000 per year, that is very difficult to accept. As self-worth is so identified with financial worth it is difficult. So, for example one extreme would be those at director levels on a six figure salary who have been made redundant for 5–6 years and want to get in at that same level. Careers are going to go across rather than up and if you look at Linda Gratton and Andrew Scott's book "A 100-year Life," they argue that you might choose different phases e.g. an intensive phase followed by a break, followed by a downwards (sideways) move, followed by a step up and to see it as a linear profession is a 20th-century review of a career.

Aviva Working Lives Report (2017) https://broker.aviva.co.uk/news/article/545/aviva-working-lives-report-2017/

Virgin money plc

Dan Perrett, Head of HR Business Partnering (Functions and Strategy Development)

At the time of this interview, in October 2017, Virgin Money was a FTSE 250 company currently employing 3,000 employees in the UK.

At the heart of everything we do is our ambition to make "everyone better off" (EBO). We aim to do this by offering good value to customers, looking after our colleagues, making a positive contribution to the communities in which we work, building positive relationships with our corporate partners and delivering sustainable profits to our shareholders. This ambition underpins our differentiated approach to banking.

Our culture is based on this ambition and sustains a virtuous circle which raises awareness of the Virgin Money brand and business as a force for good. To support this our HR policy comprises three goals: be welcoming to all, ensure a work environment where every colleague can be their true self at work and develop people to be the best they can be.

In short, whether you bank with us or work with us, we believe that all partnerships are created equal. We're a different kind of bank, which strives to treat everyone the same. And our quest to make banking better includes creating a place where all our colleagues and customers feel welcome.

In 2015, as part of the UK government's drive to improve economic productivity, Jayne-Anne Gadhia, CEO at Virgin Money, was asked to undertake a review into why women make less progress in financial services than in other industries. The review unearthed significant barriers to the progress of women and noted that breaking down such barriers would improve performance, productivity and profitability for businesses and the UK economy as a whole.

The review resulted in the Women in Finance Charter which made four key recommendations to improve gender diversity. By signing the Charter, organisations pledge to promote gender diversity by:

- Having one member of their senior executive team who is responsible and accountable for gender diversity and inclusion;
- Setting internal targets for gender diversity in senior management;
- Publishing progress annually against these targets in reports on their website; and

- Having an intention to ensure the pay of the senior executive team is linked to delivery against internal targets on gender diversity.

The Charter has resulted in more financial services firms engaging on the issue of gender diversity, and it now covers over 200 firms, employing over 650,000 people in the UK. At Virgin Money, we're passionate about fairness, equality and inclusion for men and women and, as one of the pioneers of the Charter, we made achieving gender balance a strategic priority – setting a target of 50:50 gender balance by 2020 throughout the business.

To achieve this, as well as having more women in senior management roles, we need to attract more men to customer-facing roles in our stores and contact centres.

Our 50:50 target and closing our gender pay gap are inextricably linked and that's why we decided to publish our gap well ahead of the regulatory requirement. Such transparency made for some uncomfortable headlines but once you can clearly see the shape of your business you can start to invest time and resource towards dealing with it effectively.

As a result, we have already started to move the dial. Our mean gender pay gap had reduced by 10%, to 32.5% by April 2017, and further improved to 29.7% by April 2018. We are not happy with that and we will continue to close the gap as we make further progress towards our 50:50 target.

Indeed, diversity in all its forms remains a priority as we strive to ensure that those who work for our business reflect the customers we serve, enabling us to provide a relevant, practical and personal banking service. As such, we aim to provide an environment which nurtures a high-performing, diverse and committed workforce. Beyond our work across gender, LGBT, BAME, disability and mental health, we've also signed up to the Champion for Older Worker's initiative. This is a pledge to increase the number of older people (defined as over 50 years old) we employ by 12% by 2022.

To achieve this goal, we will continue to tap into the wealth of diverse expertise and experience that older workers offer, ensure that they can access opportunities to develop and progress and, importantly, learn from the work on gender equality including publishing the number of older workers that we employ in our Annual Report. Such transparency and accountability ensures action as there's no hiding place.

Of course, creating the right culture for everyone to flourish is both a moral and economic imperative. Progressive firms recognise that unleashing the talents of the entire workforce results in benefits to business, society and the wider economy and is simply just the right thing to do.

Business in the community (BITC) the age at work campaign

Jenny Lincoln, Age Research and Policy Manager

In October 2016, Business in the Community's Leadership Team on age at work was appointed as the UK Government's "Business Champion for Older

Workers" to lead the work in supporting businesses to retain, retrain and recruit older workers.

Business in the Community (BITC) is a membership and research organisation in the UK for businesses who want to publicly demonstrate a commitment to act responsibly and invest in building a better society. It works with businesses to improve their corporate social responsibility (CSR) credentials, offers advice and tailors programmes to meet their needs.

BITC Age at Work campaign, through the mechanism of The Ageing Workforce Award, identifies those businesses that are responding to these emerging needs and in turn, are maximising organisational resilience to a growing, ageing workforce.

BITC have established a campaign focused on older workers which is based on the principle of leaving no one behind, part of the 17 UN Sustainable Development Goals (SDGs), aiming to tackle poverty, climate change and inequality. These goals represent the largest ever call for collective action by governments, institutions, businesses and citizens. To achieve the SDGs and so build a sustainable future for everyone, it is essential to develop the positive impacts of business and mitigate the negative.

BITC also campaigns for gender equality, race equality and well-being at work. However, for age and older workers the issues are very different to what we would work with for race and gender, which is concerned with equal representation and the division of wealth and power across the workplace. In this case, it is not looking at representations of power and equal pay but is more concerned with age as an amplifier of these inequalities.

From research conducted by BITC and others over the last few years, there are specific barriers that older workers face in the workplace although we need to recognise that older workers are a diverse grouping with different socio-economic positions. Nevertheless, in the workplace, they experience similar trends. Trends experienced after 50 include an increased likelihood of having caring responsibilities or being a "sandwich carer" and consequently facing additional barriers in the employment market. Older workers are also experiencing a higher probability of health issues/conditions that can make it harder to balance a full-time job. So, with an ageing demographic and workforce ageing we need to try and keep people working longer and prevent people becoming unemployed before they reach state pension age. Organisations need to adapt and respond to older workers; that is the premise of our campaign.

Japan already has an aged population as opposed to an ageing population, so they've had to deal with societal and economic impact a little bit sooner than European countries. Australian research collected a decade ago showed that a government backed incentive scheme to recruit older workers didn't work. Employers, despite the skills gap and perfect storm, didn't want to go to a specifically targeted older worker pool and it was seen that individuals didn't want to be identified as old. We are increasingly thinking that the words "old" and "older" are part of the problem and SAGA, an organisation who specialise in over 50s recently joined our leadership team and will share work with us they have done about how some older workers see themselves or perceive themselves. They might internalise subtle ageism and bias that exist within society or the external environment in that ageism has been there for so long, yet it is not really discussed and has not really been challenged in the same way as racism or sexism. So, there is possibly a confidence gap and knock-on effect of internalising that bias and affects the type of jobs people apply to. This can be even more pronounced for older female workers, who face a double disadvantage of ageism and sexism, thereby affecting their confidence even more. Biases seep into workplaces; into recruitment, management processes, appraisals and even redundancies.

Research shows gender roles are more embedded and polarised amongst older people, and men and women had fewer career options and different expectations 20/30 years ago which is reflected in the workplace today. Women who are over 50 now are much more likely to be in lower-paid/skilled work than younger women, and men of their own age. Longitudinal research from the US shows that where sectors and jobs that became feminised and female dominated over time when once male dominated, the pay relatively dropped. So, women are undervalued. They don't necessarily choose lower-paid work, it follows them where they go.

Women are not necessarily less confident, they demonstrate confidence in very different ways to men and possibly don't express it in the same way at work. If they are less confident with regards to their career ambitions, it is largely driven by their experiences of gender bias and the lower expectations put on them by society. I would question the "gender confidence gap" – men can also be overconfident.

In general, there needs to be a different approach to changing careers away from one job for life up the ladder. A BITC member company talks of a climbing wall, as opposed to a ladder, giving more opportunities for people to move across and around the organisation and sectors as opposed to the climbing wall of moving up and so removing the pressure to just keep climbing up. If it's such a big part of your identity and if you no longer have that opportunity you perceive that as a negative thing, then going down a level is something people don't always want to do. Careers are going to become more like this though.

There is lots of research showing older workers are less likely to take up training but also less likely to be offered it by employers. BITC recently conducted research which indicates the same trend. In addition, our research found that older workers don't see the same value in traditional training formats as the young. Their preference is for on-the-job learning to one-off training programmes, and they want to see a tangible impact and value to them. If they don't see a tangible benefit of how it will affect their day-to-day job, then they're less likely to take up offers of training compared to younger workers. There may be other research that has different interpretations of that.

People will want to move about more and change a bit more. The younger generation are preparing for that from the get-go. And work is increasingly more insecure anyway (short-term work, internships, temporary jobs) and for the 50+ people that concept of multiple careers didn't really exist when they entered work. But they're now having to work for longer and perhaps unlearn some of those cultural norms. Employers and employees alike need to think about how to retrain and reskill, particularly for those in lower-skilled work that are more likely to be made redundant though digitalisation. This will be crucial for a key vulnerable set of older workers and retraining is going to be increasingly important – there must be a Plan B.

It's important for all ages. It goes back to having autonomy and not being treated like a child by employers and having a say in your own development. That correlates with older workers being less likely to have that conversation, offered training and even have that dialogue to begin with.

The Ageing Workforce Award through BITC http://awards.bitc.org.uk/rb-awards-2018/the-ageing-workforce-award

Published with permission from an interview (2017) with Jenny Lincoln, Age Research and Policy Manager at Business in the Community.

RiseSmart Australia and New Zealand

Catriona Byrne, Creative Director, RiseSmart Australia and New Zealand

Older workers – diversity, ageing and workforce management

Sage is a niche consultancy formed 13 years ago and now forms part of RiseSmart, a US career transition company. Sage delivers their career transitions programmes, consulting in ageing and workforce management. It takes a holistic view of transitions and portfolio careers and recognised that this area was the next big thing. Organisations could see that an enormous volume of baby boomers were leaving the workforce but then the baby boomers stayed on in the workplace, as over time their retirement savings had disappeared. Organisations realised that people wanted to work differently. The central premise of Sage's business is that many people in the demographic 50–55+ range, with retirement in the offing, and where the current retirement age in Australia is 59 and creeping up, do not necessarily want to retire in the same way that retirement has traditionally been presented but were very happy to work but in a different way which offered challenges and opportunities.

Challenge and opportunities for demography shift

The number one challenge is that retirement is a strong paradigm for people and there is a sense that you work full-time and retire full-time. When discussing diversity, it is not just age, but diversity within that demographic. That is whole diversity within demographics and we see sweeping wide statements about what older workers want.

But it's important to look at gender, and within that, it is different for blue collar with a physical load versus white collar as there is a difference in reskilling. For example, one of my clients is a plumber who worked for a water facility said, "the day my knees give out that's the day I'll retire." So, there is a different answer for a white-collar worker in an office or a knowledge worker. Recognising that diversity within the demographic is very important, so it's important to challenge the notion of retirement and that retirement itself is not a helpful word as it means withdrawing.

So, people want to work longer but they need to work differently. They may want flexible hours, or to use knowledge differently, or use the same knowledge in a different sector, or in a different way in project-type work or managing paid work and volunteering. So, we're about challenging the sense of full-time retirement that I stop full-time and withdraw.

It's not anymore that "I stop full-time and withdraw and go play golf." So, how do we attract a large pool of talent workers? The challenge for workers is to think about retirement differently and the challenge for organisations is to think about roles that can attract this large talent pool of very able workers that they might not have thought of before.

They don't have the younger pool of graduates, so the shift means they can't keep recruiting talent from a younger pool as they are not there. Also, the careers are different. Someone in a new role starting at 45 can be a long-term worker with 20 or 30 years of work. e.g. the LSE 100-year life concept book. We need to rethink the impact of longevity, of how people think about work. That is, recognising the diversity in the demographic and challenge notions of retirement.

Much is geared to the retirement age. Superannuation and insurance is geared to 65 as it was thought people didn't live much longer then. People can live 20 years healthily after work, and still have a great capacity for work. All these structures have assumptions that 65 is the turning point. So, there's a lot of structural stuff to challenge. In all our work it is helping people to think differently about what retirement looks like. And we are often asked if we will do retirement intention surveys when really the question to ask if you want people to work longer is "Do you want work intention surveys asking what the next 20 years of work looks like for you?" and you'd get a very different answer.

Also, we need to think differently about what talent looks like. So, it's about changing and turning the whole notion upside down about what ageing looks like in the workplace.

Diverse workforces mean that, and there is lots of research around age diversity in the workplace, different life experiences are represented at the table and strong arguments to reflect your customer base. For example, in insurance where there's an older demographic of customer; older persons would build rapport and can offer life experience. Also, there is diversity for diversity of thought. Additionally, reflecting society in your workplace is a healthy way to be getting balance and diversity of thought and longer-term studies support that.

Learning and development

Who is not ageing? What you are saying for an ageing workforce speaks to the whole workforce and is equally relevant to each age band. The Human Rights Commission in Australia uses the term older worker, as older is relative. In some organisations it might be 45 and others 70.

For older workers when thinking about learning and development, several financial institutions and banks have won awards from US AAARP (a large membership organisation) for age friendly workplaces. One of them, Westpac, had a recruitment campaign for older workers where they learned that it was optimum to use the same Learning and Development programme as for other workers, just that it required a bit more time for IT. For example, it was extended from a 3-day to a 5-day course giving older workers an equal chance. Also, in the recruitment process older age groups need slightly more time as an adaptive requirement.

Regarding technology, we find that the older demographic is the fastest take up of social media, iPads etc., so the stereotyping does not quite ring true, but the review point is to adapt and think of the point that if you didn't grow up with Excel and Microsoft Word how would you adapt? Change the pace, but you would adapt, that's what you would do with every generation. So, development can be blended, face to face and an online model hybrid model can be offered. It's the same but amplified, so adapting what you have already got, which is the same as other diversity cohorts, e.g. the visually impaired. There are many ways to adapt.

Knowledge transfer

We see that older workers like both formal and tacit learning programmes but in our experience, we haven't seen anything different between the generations. There is an appetite for collegial and peer working where you share knowledge in a slightly structured way. Having multigenerational learning and learning circles – both older and younger people get energised by that.

I think recognition of prior learning and life experiences is very important, that it is important to challenge assumptions. Particularly say, when you are creating a career as a woman coming back into the workforce who has managed a family for 15 years, volunteering in school so having administrative and organisational skills. So, we need to look at what learning is there, skills and what they already know and not assume anything. We always encourage people to present their skills in that way whether it is paid work or volunteer. It's about being able to articulate accomplishments confidently.

You will always get ageist attitudes. We say, its often not about age, it's about attitudes. In any workplace, it's important as workers we have a positive attitude and are confident in our own skills and give an idea of depth of experience. As far as job searching in late career is concerned, the difference is that many people have often had one or two jobs with long tenure in one organisation or field and have not undertaken the job seeking preparation process which you can pick up. On the other hand, the younger generation are very familiar with ten different roles by the time they're 30. It's really important that older workers have career planning and searching skills, do not hold back on their life experiences e.g. running a Scout group for 20 years, working with many stakeholders and that they can join the dots for the employers and be confident that there are transferable skills that can apply to many situations. It doesn't always work but it doesn't mean you shouldn't do it.

Intergenerational learning

We've seen reverse e-mentoring using younger generations typically to help with LinkedIn, social media, Facebook, working with Word, Excel and learning circles, so we've seen intergenerational learning with that. We've run 300 knowledge transfer (KT) programmes, using typically a "sage," someone identified who has the skills and knowledge and is well acknowledged in the organisation as a knowledge holder, and run learning circles. Also, we encourage midcareer people to, say, structure an audio interview or write a FAQ type of document going around the organisation. Or through learning circles with Socratic questioning, where the "sage" starts off and then gets the younger ones to ask the questions. So, a real multigenerational approach across the workforce.

It's organic and we make it intentional; some may be structured, or some might be discussing management skills, which is looser, to create learning. We're getting the dialogue through and people take the learning that they take. The KT multi-intergenerational programme gives permission to seek knowledge and for people to create their own learning and ask the questions. Typically, older workers are very happy to share knowledge and don't often have the opportunity to do it in a helpful, structured way so the more avenues that we can give to share the knowledge productively is very healthy way from a learning perspective.

I think older workers can very much feel vulnerable and much of our work has been challenging organisations in saying what structures might make them feel vulnerable. For instance, when recruiting, on your website what faces are reflected, are they all young faces, when you have older people of fifty that want to apply? Do you have older women reflected? In a large focus group, one woman said, "I feel invisible." So, what are you doing to ensure that the way that you reflect your workplace is diverse, such as reward and recognition programmes? Are the older generations reflected and suited for a range of ages? All of these areas; the way you hire, track, promote and how people leave the organisations reflecting working lives needs attention. They're often not big things, just needing tweaks. Such as having Grandparents Day. What can you do to increase the visibility of older workers in your organisation? And knowledge exchange is one thing that can be done. Staff feel vulnerable when things are geared to a certain age group. Often it is unconscious. The question to ask organisations is "Are you thinking about it"?

There is a mind shift between an organisational responsibility for your career development and your own responsibility. In the past, there was a paternal view that career path and all training was provided, sometimes that didn't include women. Now, you are responsible for your personal brand, the way you present yourself, you create your own opportunities. Making sure that you're proactive and skilled in that area is really important. Things like managing your own LinkedIn profile. When we run career transition programmes we run courses around creating online profiles to enhance your career. What do you want to do differently, and it's a mindset shift, increasingly people recognise that but if you've spent forty years in one environment you haven't had to worry about growing your own career and can we change that?

Catriona Byrne, Creative Director and cofounder of Sageco – ageing workforce specialists (acquired by Randstad and rebranded as RiseSmart in 2017)

Royal Society for the encouragement of arts, manufactures and commerce (RSA), Future of Work Centre

Benedict Dellot, Head of the RSA Future Work Centre, and Associate Director, Economy, Enterprise and Manufacturing, RSA

The mission of the RSA, UK (Royal Society for the encouragement of Arts, Manufactures and Commerce) is to enrich society through ideas and action. Its Future of Work Centre was set up in 2018.

We could have looked at many areas when launching Future of Work Centre, e.g. work, change, etc., but we chose to concentrate on long-term technology where there would be the biggest change to workers, whether someone is employed in a conventional, permanent or gig economy job. We are attempting to broaden our focus not just on AI and robotics but on "bread and butter" technologies, e.g. smart phones, digitisation and the shift to virtual platforms, such as in books and music. Now, by using smart phones we can correspond at all hours which eats into work–life balance, so a new vacuum is being filled, eroding leisure time. So, we're not just looking at dazzling technology but more the day-to-day work.

Our USP goes beyond just the impact of technology on jobs and availability, but on levels of recruitment and surveillance. So, that represents a wide-angled lens in the debate.

Our aim is to:

a) Understand what the big challenges are facing workers. So, for example, the good work gap with stagnating wages which could be due to work intensification. Everyone is working more intensively in the hours that they do work, harder and faster in hours of work.
b) Technology – we're trying to understand what impact technology will have on work.
c) We want to work out how to update the social contract – that is the divisions and rights, expectations and responsibilities between employers,

state and workers around areas such as sick pay, holiday pay, maternity pay and asking who pays.

There are different models here (1) all up to the individual, (2) asking more from consumers through the national tax system for those who aren't employed, for example, the self-employed, and (3), should we be asking people to pay for these to ensure that good work is prevailing in the future?

Learning

I think that the principle here is whether we can learn to live with low-skilled work and whether we can professionalise it, possibly through technology. For example, what does a social care worker's job look like in 2030, where their roles can be expanded on from low-skilled work (e.g. removing heavy lifting, back-breaking work) due to increased professionalisation through augmentation. And then how do we ensure it is a career and that people can expand the capability within that job. We're not just coming at it as helping to escape low-skilled work to high-skills job. Low-skilled work will be around for the near-to-medium term and will continue to exist.

We have many further questions to answer. How do we make new kinds of work and learn to live with it? We need to think about employability for these jobs and the curriculum. We need to think more laterally about how employees can be financed and be encouraged to continue learning throughout their working lives. We need to think about what employers need to do to bring out the best in their workers.

We're trying to work out if learning should be much more individualised rather than employer led. There is an apprenticeship levy where every employer can dip into a pot. While it is a good idea, the problem is that it is quite "old school" in the types of training employers are obliged to provide and it is not available if someone is self-employed or in intermittent employment.

France, for example, has a lifelong learning fund which is attached to an individualised personal training account with every worker in charge of their training. We're looking at how do you expand the quality and deepen lifelong learning? We concentrate on post school adult learning, that is post 21+ years. Regardless of existing skills sets, what will people be needing?

We're also looking at how to accelerate the adoption of these technologies for productivity and business competitivity. How we do so is on our own terms and the terms of workers as we at the RSA think new technologies are a positive thing which increases productivity. We are on the side of the workers, but we are also pragmatic. Lifelong learning is one of the major levers of intervention and change for us. Another is in tax and welfare and worker voice looking at the future of trade unions. A further fourth area is employer practice to support workers.

Framework

Digital reskilling and upskilling is the easy job and many companies are involved in it e.g. the Barclays Apprenticeship scheme. I believe that upskilling is not the area that needs most attention. It is not the biggest challenge. The major task is the reinsertion of people into the new workplaces. The difficulty is helping people fit into new careers that are growing and those that are declining. We are leaving bricks and mortar, so, it is different jobs, higher-skilled jobs, use of technology and new jobs in the experience sector that we will see, for example, in physiotherapy and personal trainers.

There will be different time frames for different technologies; the move to self-drive cars in possibly 15 years, to e-commerce which is already here, possibly 10 years.

The Fourth Industrial Revolution covers different technologies such as blockchain, the Internet of things, sensors applied to physical goods, virtual reality etc. I don't believe it will be mass automation, but it will be very gradual. If one organisation doesn't move across then another will then, and it will affect market share, and business competitiveness in a free market. The most productive will race ahead, we have already seen that with the big technology players such as Amazon, Google, Facebook and Apple. They have the technology at their fingertips to move into different markets if they wish.

RSA Future of Work Centre

www.thersa.org/action-and-research/rsa-projects/economy-enterprise-manufacturing-folder/the-future-of-work

Apprentice retraining for the Civil Service on their three-year apprenticeship scheme

Jo Hall, Apprentice

After university, I worked in finance for a local health authority for three years before retraining as a teacher. I taught for over 20 years, finally handing in my notice about three years ago, due to lots of contributory factors to do with the changing nature of the job and also the increased stress of coping for a few months when my partner was working away from home in the week. Initially, I did an Royal Horticulture Society (RHS) horticulture course just because I wanted to, and I had the time. I really enjoyed it and achieved a Level 2 RHS Diploma. I looked at some relevant jobs, but the hours were tricky with a family. I thought about setting up on my own tidying gardens but was still lacking in confidence and I know that I am not very good at selling myself.

Not keen to return to the stress of teaching, I started applying for other jobs in school like learning mentor/pastoral roles and 1:1 with SEN pupils. With financial pressures in schools, these jobs are becoming increasingly scarce or are for much more limited hours. I worked as a supply cover for hospital education, but again this was limited hours, so I began to consider a return to finance work. I started applying for various posts and was disappointed that my transferable skills from teaching were not valued by potential employers as much as recent work experience. I realised that I really had no choice but to start right at the bottom again. Being 50, I felt that I really needed to get on with some qualifications to progress as quickly as possible. I was considering self-study at home when I came across information about apprenticeships which seemed to have so many advantages.

I applied to the three-year apprenticeship Civil Service (Defence Equipment and Support). I am studying AAT (Accounts Technician) one day a week at South Gloucestershire and Stroud College in Bristol. The qualification for an Accounts technician is a bookkeeping and costing one and then I go off and work for myself. At 50 it's very exciting to be starting something new. With a group of apprentices, we have fun together. In a group of 24, there is a mixed intake from all the apprentice schemes I'm on, half are school leavers, a quarter from university and five are much older. It's great to have the work experience and I don't have to study at home and I get paid leave and study leave. I will get experience in different parts of the business, so I will have two/three areas I have covered.

Barriers in being an older worker as an apprentice?

I find everyone is very friendly and I feel part of it. It's strange being in a classroom again but in work placements I found it much easier than the younger ones; we were more confident. Being older made the workplace experience easier and we can chat easily. The younger ones are either intimidated or worried they don't have anything in common with people. I expect they're fine in their teams, but I had more confidence than I expected. But that might be me that I'm lucky with that and some may find it harder. I don't see much difference in the role of the older worker and lots of people have work experience they can share and probably a more balanced perspective experience and can remain calmer and not worry about things, although this is not true of all people. If you've been through life's up and downs you can work out what's important. If there's a deadline looming or whatever you may find it easier to prioritise. I feel a bit of a "mum" to some of the young apprenticeships! It's a nice relationship. Older people can disappear but I'm not finding that's where I am.

Transferable skills not recognised when job hunting

When I came to write CVs and presented my skills to other organisations they didn't seem relevant, but the work experience was valued much more. It wasn't about whether you were a quick learner. To be honest, I think that is why I was lucky with the Civil Service as the application process is very much looking at skills and competencies and online tests. None of it was looking at your experience to get through to the interview stage. That was lucky, I'm not sure how I'd get on in another sector when applying. It makes you think about university applications in getting rid of bias.

I think older women feel more vulnerable. In teaching now, for the first few years your experience is really valuable then you reach a certain level as you've been doing it for years, people don't think you're going to get much better, they think you're outdated with techniques, a bit old. To a certain extent, you can book yourself onto training if your managers agree it is relevant to your work. Before there wasn't the money for it.

Having started doing my accountancy course at college I'm really glad that I am not doing it at home by self-studying as I would have found it very hard. I don't particularly like online learning which the young are used to. There are more videos which are easier to follow. I like the opportunity to discuss things as well, something interactive. That kind of texting forum where people become friends through messages ... I'm more used to face to face, it's partly personality and partly age.

People I come into contact with on the apprenticeship scheme are very open and it is interesting learning alongside the younger ones. Some of them having done A-level economics or business studies, have already picked up a lot of the skills we're learning, they've been helpful in sharing the useful tips they've learned in a helpful way. Being older we can offer more to do with being in a workplace, being with other people, how to access resources and help or how they can ask or who to approach in various things.

At the beginning, we had quite of a lot of activities working together so that really helped. Interestingly, they split apprenticeships into two halves. We do then tend to split automatically into these groups, so not across the ages, but people you spent time with. Technology is not too much of an issue as its standard Office, Microsoft Excel, etc. Nothing too whizzy.

In terms of career promotion, hopefully, it is open to all. The idea is we will stay on, but they don't guarantee it. They've said in the past that some haven't done very well and that previous apprenticeships haven't necessarily been experienced. Interestingly, they've taken on older people this year than previous years and they're starting to realise the benefits. I only heard this through the students. There's a group of young ones going out every night whereas someone my age is far more likely to stay in.

They're (Civil Service) doing it as they've got a shortfall but I'm not sure they'll carry on recruiting at the same rate as they have had several schemes running at same time and doing a fast track at a higher level too, so they've currently got more than one apprenticeship scheme. At the moment, I'd stay on if it was offered to me, but I haven't seen much yet.

There is no particular differentiation for old workers, we're all doing the same thing. In a way you are a bit rejuvenated and it's being given the time to try something completely different and it's a safe place to try it. If you're an apprentice there should be support if you struggle. I haven't needed to test that yet. Apart from going from a relatively good salary right to the bottom again, I thought I would arrive more quickly through an apprenticeship scheme than taking a job going in at entry level and getting the experience. You never know in smaller work places you could be recognised but I'm not sure. As a second career I don't want to hang around. Three years as an older person does not feel like a long time.

A case study of underutilised talent and lack of strategic human resource management and planning for older workers

Dr Max Coates, UCL

Robert had worked for a local authority for over 25 years. A graduate in civil engineering he had specialised at a post-graduate level in water management. Not surprisingly, in a deluge/drought water economy his expertise had been much in demand over many years. At a personal level he is meticulous by style and tends to be an isolate in terms of his personality.

The local authority for which he worked had been subject to a number of boundary changes, merges with other authorities and diet of continuous internal reorganisation. Some years ago, the strata above his pay grade was the focus of a criminal investigation into contract fraud. This turbulence had meant that there was an inconsistency in much of the line management within his department. Managerial interactions were almost exclusively linked to task and offered little in terms of a wider dimension of either professional development or motivational support.

As Robert entered the twilight of his career, he has now retired, his contribution to work became minimalist and his personal attitude ever more cynical. To a large extent this was driven by a foreshortened personal career horizon and an attitude by the organisation which tended to view him as a knowledge bank which needed depleting before he finally retired.

Budgetary constraints within the organisation significantly reduced the opportunities for CPD. Much that was on offer was to meet mandatory requirements such as health and safety, safeguarding and communicate policy change. What little additional CPD that was available was focused on younger workers. The local authority's HR department offered a few courses on the "preparing for retirement" ticket. Ironically, the latter increased Robert's feelings of alienation.

Much of his professional career had been framed by long-term environmental targets within the 15- to 20-year bracket. Government legislation was now constraining strategy to a much more immediate timescale. Much of the strategy development was being undertaken by the "young turks" who spasmodically utilised Robert's insights on an almost consultancy basis. This fuelled his increasing belief that he was more of a commodity more than a contributor to the department.

Robert had found the final phase of his career to be disappointing with retirement described in terms of escape rather than being seen as a welcomed transition. For probably 10 years his line management experience had been about task accountability with little if any evidence of concern for him as an employee. CPD was seldom available and what was on offer seldom played to his motivational needs as a technical expert.

It was interesting to note that as he left there was no institutional celebration of his departure. Robert actually saw this as a good thing. Almost as a postscript, it is worth noting that Robert was not entering this phase of his life alone. He has been married for many years. His partner had also encountered parallel problems within her organisation as she approached retirement. They began to feed on each other's negative emotions. Their conversations reinforcing their respective perceptions and attitudes towards work.

Reflections on yoga for well-being in older life

Sarah Tucker, yoga practitioner, author and travel journalist

As someone who is 53 (so in the older age bracket), I qualified to teach yoga because I am a teacher and a storyteller. As a novelist and radio and TV broadcaster, I understand the power of the voice – not only what you say but more importantly how you say it. In radio, people listen to how you say something and then what you say. They listen to the vibration. So, when I teach yoga, I choose my words carefully and story tell while the class lay in savasana (on their backs, eyes closed, palms facing up). I use repetition a lot. I use colour. I use imagery. I use journeys. I do exactly the same thing with the children I teach from 3–18, only with the younger ones I don't call it "meditation" which sounds far too much like medication for their liking, but "close-your-eyes stories" which is exactly what meditation is.

By fifty, most are reconsidering their lives. They are looking back and looking forward. The men are usually in midlife crisis and women are in menopause (yoga is extremely good for menopause as it assists with balancing hormones). They may still be on a path of material gain, regardless of how much they have already. But usually, 9 times out of 10, they are in a state of nonacceptance. They are stiff with judgement, regret, hate, anger, remorse, loneliness and grief. All of these come from fear. Fear is the opposite of love. We hold fear in our bodies, unless we let it go. Culturally we are not allowed to let it go because then we are vulnerable and culturally it is not good to be vulnerable – especially if you are a man. Women are "allowed" to show fear through tears, and men are allowed to show fear through anger. Both are positive releases of emotion, but neither gender has been taught how to release the other emotion. So, by the time they turn fifty, women are full of anger and men are full of sadness and neither know how to release it. That's where yoga comes in – and the storytelling. Once they know how to breathe from the belly and they are able to accept themselves and have compassion for themselves and most importantly learn to like themselves (most 50 pluses do not), they are able to release emotions which are held in their body. In many cases this is an emotional tsunami. This is why they don't want to release for fear of this tsunami. Anger internalised is depression. Inability to handle stress causes a multitude of issues – one of which is cancer. Our inability to deal with stress causes cancer. But the body is like an onion and will release the emotion one stage at a time.

My observations with teaching yoga to the over fifties are three-fold.

Children do not deal with things well. I mention children although this is about fifty pulses because children store their emotion – their grief, their anger, their loneliness in their cells. It becomes part of their DNA. (What is said to them when they are young impacts on their later lives). This is why social media and religion has always had such an impact. Religions "hold on lightly and pull back tightly" and the impact is always felt in later life. We hold guilt in our body. Many religions base their fervour on guilt. And we teach our children guilt. This may serve the community, but it is bad for our bodies. We also teach them how to make others feel guilty. That is like teaching them how to inflict wounds on others. Much better to teach a sense of responsibility for the self. And to focus on the self, like the self, believe in the self. To empower the self.

All of the emotional issues I deal with, with over fifties, originate from childhood. *All of them.*

Fifty somethings. They are inflexible in opinion as they are in body. They hear what they want to hear. They project what they want to see and hear. They predetermine the storyline. They prejudge others and above all themselves. They are full of judgement and guilt. They have predetermined opinions. They are not open minded. This is understandable, but means they judge rather than observe. Judgement closes the ability to communicate and learn down. Observing opens one up all the time to new learning. Reading back this paragraph I know this sounds very harsh, but it is observing this age group for the past four years and it is this way because this is their defence mechanism.

They are masters of passive aggressive. As a travel journalist, I have witnessed the impact of culture on the emotions of each nationality where I have travelled and on the gender dynamic. But the passive aggressive is used in my experience globally. So, when something is said which is hurtful, but it is said in a gentle way, the body is being attacked but people are confused because it appears to be said in a kind way. What also makes this worse is that narcissists use self-help books to manipulate others. If you like, they are using them as a tool book on how to compete with others.

The key to all of this is to listen to the breath. To breathe from the belly and to focus on listening to the body, to trusting the instinct, to believing in the instinct. Animals and children have this already. If you like, they are the inner child.

Case studies of older people and yoga

53-year-old man.

Came to class with his wife. Financially functional, materially successful, Not a team player. Horrendous lower back problems. Played a lot of sport but was getting a lot of lower back pain. At the beginning, he stayed at the back (most people do because they don't want to not look good as they don't know the poses, but it is in fact better to come up front). Gradually as he gained more confidence he moved forward until he was almost next to me. He was unable to touch his toes and didn't like to do backbends and was incapable of any form of twist. I have visualisations which work with particular issues. One is to do with releasing anger, another grief, another moving on, another letting go and so on. Through the practice of vinyasa (flowing from one asana to another) he was able to release the lower back tension. In men this is where they hold anger. He was unable to let go of the anger, which was based on his inability to "control" the loss of his brother. Not being a team player meant also he had issues with trust and an inability to communicate. So ultimately, he was also lonely and grieving for loss of trust. Behind the anger was grief. Men stick at anger because it is an easier emotion for them to express than getting to grief. Once this was overcome he could reach acceptance, and even by saying those words "I accept myself" while focusing on his breathing, he was able to let go of his grief and move on (backbend) and let go (forward bend) and twist (release deep emotions). After three months, he started seeing a reflexologist which compliments yoga practice well.

54-year-old woman.

Constant headaches, migraine, insomnia, menopausal. All tension was around the shoulders, neck and jaw, where we hold judgement – not of others although it may lead to that, but to ourselves. "Tight lipped, weight on our shoulders, stiff upper lip" our language tells us what the matter is and why we have the issues we have. We practiced a lot of backbends and open-heart postures to enable her to feel more compassion towards herself. To forgive and accept herself. It strengthened her core to believe in herself and her root chakras to make her feel safe to express herself and release her anger but in a constructive way (she took up kick-boxing!). Yoga works in harmony with many other exercise forms – and I always recommend one other type of exercise to compliment yoga. People should not just do yoga – yoga complements other therapies. I introduced aromatherapy oils to her practice – geranium and bergamot particularly balancing for hormones and menopause. After a month coming to class weeks, headaches, gone, sleeping better and hot sweats were reduced. I advised also that she stop sugar, wheat and dairy in her diet.

51-year-old man – former tennis pro.

Management consultant ironically who had anger management issues. Irritable. Unable to concentrate, memory loss. Tennis is like middle-class boxing. It is not a team sport and those who take part do not have a team mentality. They are street fighters in tennis whites. Most of the tennis pros I teach have anger management issues which mean they have very tight lower backs and flexibility is impaired. With men, the scientific has to be explained, why things are working and one part of the body impacts on the other part of the body. No mention of chakras or nadis. They are not interested in the spiritual element and will see it as something that works because it has been scientifically proven (and not the other way around). They also have an ego issue to overcome and making themselves vulnerable is challenging because their ego overrides the wish to learn (they know better). I focus on developing their flexibility and range of movement. A lot of balancing (which strengthens courage) because it needs courage to make yourself vulnerable. Then a lot of heart opening postures (triangle and camel pose). Then the stretching which allows them to release. This gentleman became very tearful in the stretches which is normal for men when releasing anger. So, a lot of child pose (head down) which is very restorative and also hides the tears. (I always have a box of tissues in the room when I work on heart chakras). His issue was with his mother, and always aiming to please people who were impossible to please (like his mother). After two months coming twice a week, he started working with a kinesiologist as well and sound therapy.

In summation, yoga is a tool (not THE tool) to helping women with menopause and men in emotional crisis (which usually comes out in their bodies). It is an accessible way of women and most importantly men engaging with their emotions but looking as though they are doing it to "deal with stress" rather than something deeper. Our inability to deal with our emotions has physical consequences. *Our emotions impact on our body not the other way around.* This generation was taught by their parents to hold stuff in – and that emotions are messy. But that has consequences. Cancer is caused by our inability to deal with stress – not by stress itself. When we hit fifty – bang – we burst with the emotional tsunami which has built up since childhood, and it shows in our bodies and our behaviour in all different ways. Stress is caused by fear of the known and unknown. Overcoming fear requires courage and compassion, not only by the individual but also those who are aiming to change the culture of fear. In the meantime, I'm teaching yoga in schools and campaigning to get it on the curriculum – because it's a start.

Chapter 6 discusses the future of work and workplaces and explores some implications for later life learning.

Reference

Aviva Working Lives Report (2017) https://broker.aviva.co.uk/news/article/545/aviva-working-lives-report-2017/

6 The future of work

This chapter considers future work landscapes, the role of older workers in this landscape and the forms of learning and skills which they will potentially require. It also explores holistic notions of well-being in the workplace necessary to support older workers, whom, as has been presented in this book will increasingly play a significant part in workforces due to demographic changes.

Skills development is among the greatest global challenges facing countries, enterprises and people (Deloitte 2017). Crucially, it plays a vital role in promoting employment, economic growth and inclusive societies. This necessitates the combining of the resources of the workplace and education to realise and partner suitable training and development opportunities for all throughout their careers to realise sustained growth and innovation through an improved labour market (Skills for Employment n.d.).

In 2009, G20 Leaders called on the International Labour Organisation (ILO) to establish a training strategy to support strong, sustainable and balanced growth across all G20 countries. Working with employers, employees, OECD and UNESCO the strategy was taken forward in the form of the Training Strategy submitted to the Toronto G20 Summit in June 2010 and included in the Action Plan on Development adopted at the Seoul G20 Summit later that year. The Training Strategy called on international organisations to work together to support developing countries, in particular low-income countries, "to continue to develop employment-related skills that are better matched to employer and market needs in order to attract investment and decent jobs" (IOE BIAC 2010:7).

Intended as a framework for developing a suitably skilled workforce for the future and ultimately for obtaining decent work in sustainable enterprises, the Training Strategy addressed strategic issues and identifies the critical elements or "building blocks" for connecting education and training to the world of work (ibid.).

At the 2010 G20 Business Strategy meeting on Lifelong Learning (IOE, BIAC 2010) it was declared that:

> Business strongly supports the creation of a Global Training Strategy to respond to the current financial and jobs crises and also to adapt labour markets from the long-term perspective.
>
> (IOE BIAC 2010:1)

And:

> The strategy urges G20 governments to enhance delivery of lifelong learning and employability to ensure that the needs of companies and learners are better served, especially by ensuring; access to quality education and vocational training for all; matching education and training to the needs of the labour market with a systemic capacity to respond to change; employability and flexibility during one's whole professional life; continuous improvement of skills training systems.
>
> (ibid:7)

The business strategy meeting also urged governments to "take a particular commitment to the skills development and training needed to re-equip job seekers over 45 taking account of an ageing population in most countries" (ibid:7).

Among the 2010 Business Strategy recommendations for governments, employers and individuals was the call that:

> Governments should aim for simple, transparent user friendly education and training systems while facilitating and supporting a culture of lifelong learning which emphasised that employers should train and retrain employees; advocate continuous improvement in education and training; identify current and forecast training needs and provide training opportunities to employees internally or through training providers.
>
> (ibid:8)

The Strategy also views it incumbent on employees to take responsibility for their own learning:

> Employees should access continuing training; to take initiative and invest in themselves to develop transferable skills and competencies that are not job or employer specific; to pursue a career and lifelong employability, recognising this may include work in different industries and with different employers and to be flexible and adaptable to the use of new technologies and processes.
>
> (IOE, BIAC 2010:14)

More recently, the ILO (2018) reports that globally, people aged 65+ are projected to account for 11.7% of the total population in 2030 and 15.8% in 2050, from 9.3% in 2017. The ageing of the population will be particularly acute in Europe, Northern America and Eastern Asia. This means that by 2030, the number of people aged 65+ in the high-income regions of Northern, Southern and Western Europe will be equivalent to 55% of its labour force, increased from 42% in 2017 (p. 46). Additionally, in key emerging markets such as China and the Russian Federation, the labour force is expected to drop substantially while the elderly population is expected to increase rapidly. However, there are some regions, such as Africa and Southern Asia, which still have very substantial young populations entering the labour force, so the challenge is for adequate job creation for this group (ibid.).

Moreover, ageing populations will add further pressure to future labour market challenges which will test workers' ability to keep up with the pace of innovation and structural changes in labour markets. Globally, the average age of the labour force is expected to rise from nearly 40 in 2017 to 41 in 2030, growing considerably faster in Europe and Eastern Asia, notably China (ILO 2018:3). Thus:

> Fostering the employability of workers through lifelong learning is key to expanding their employment opportunities, also at an older age. Targeted actions are also needed to encourage older workers' participation in training and skills-updating schemes in order to help lower the risk of labour market detachment and early retirement which would put added pressure on pension systems.
>
> (ibid:3)

The 2018 ILO report concludes:

> Therefore, the ageing of the labour force calls for greater efforts to maintain and update older workers' skills, with the aim of ensuring that they are able to shift sectors and occupations when structural changes alter the composition of jobs in the labour market. In this regard, it is particularly important that countries take prompt action to foster the employability of workers throughout their working lives, with a view to expanding their employment opportunities at an older age.
>
> (ILO 2018:48)

The Fourth Industrial Revolution – new technologies, processes and structures

Advances in biological sciences, neuroscience and IT are leading the way to the Fourth Industrial Revolution (Schwab 2016). The first industrial revolution, through the development of machinery which replaced manpower, demanded new skills to operate the new machinery, culminating in advances in manufacture. The second industrial age demanded further specialised skills and management of repetitive work. In the digital revolution some repetitive jobs are becoming redundant, whereas, higher cognitive skills in nonroutine cognitive roles requiring interaction with others are increasingly valued.

The UK's Taylor Review of Modern Working Practices (2017), thereafter the Taylor Review, drawing on Frey and Osborne's (2013) work suggests that with rapid advances in artificial intelligence and machine leaning routine cognitive jobs that are not usually performed by the lowest-skilled workers are also being automated in addition to service-related routine tasks, leading to a decrease in middle-income roles and a "hollowing out" of jobs. But in contrast, high-income cognitive jobs and low-income manual occupations have grown. Frey and Osborne's summary into findings of their research into how susceptible jobs are to computerisation indicate that:

> Our findings thus imply that as technology races ahead, low-skill workers will reallocate to tasks that are nonsusceptible to computerisation i.e., tasks requiring creative and social intelligence. For workers to win the race, however, they will have to acquire creative and social skills.
>
> (Frey and Osborne 2013:45)

Price Waterhouse and Cooper (PwC) have documented scenarios for possible futures for workplaces moving to 2022 (PwC 2014) and 2030 (PwC 2018), envisaging four scenarios where all indicate an increasing use of technology to assist, augment and replace human work. And all depend on digital technology to link talent pools and customers and create financially beneficial relationships between individuals, organisations or groups of people.

Nevertheless, not all is doom-mongering. The PwC report (2014) suggests:

> By replacing workers doing routine, methodical tasks, machines can amplify the comparative advantage of those workers with problem-solving, leadership, emotional intelligence, empathy and creativity skills.
>
> (PwC 2014:7)

Thus, automation will by no means replace a human workforce in the foreseeable future. And there is space for value in that higher-level cognitive skills are need in creativity, innovation, imagination and design skills for the roles that automation cannot reach. Such employees having those skills will be extremely valued by employers. It is that intellectual capital that organisations will need to survive and flourish and keep them ahead of the competition.

Additionally, both the structure of work and the type of workforce is changing. Robotics, sensors, artificial intelligence (AI) and cognitive computing are now mainstream, alongside what is an open talent economy for those who are in demand. The Deloitte report (2017) on global trends "The Future of Work" discusses an augmented workforce as increasingly diversified.

> Companies can no longer consider their workforce to be only the employees on their balance sheet but must include freelancers, "gig economy" workers and crowds. These on- and off-balance-sheet workers are being augmented with machines and software. Together, these trends

> will result in the redesign of almost every job, as well as a new way of thinking about workforce planning and the nature of work.
>
> (2017:9)

The report found that change is well underway with 41% of respondents to the Deloitte annual survey have either fully implemented or made significant process in adopting cognitive and AI technologies, with a further 35% reporting pilot programmes. This change will require a learning and development organisation that can deliver learning, that is always on and always available, over a range of mobile platforms (Deloitte 2017).

Nevertheless, the predictions about the job losses that will be incurred through automation vary widely in predictions as the Taylor Review (2017) notes drawing our attention to the Deloitte research that over the period 2010–2015, automation has created approximately four times as many jobs as it has lost.

The landscape of the future workforce

Undoubtedly though technological change will impact on work and types of employment and we need to be able to adapt, but technology can also offer new opportunities for smarter regulation, more flexible entitlements and new ways for people to organise (Taylor Review 2017).

The International Labour Organization (ILO 2018) points out that despite the undoubted shape and scope of the workforce and its global impact there will not just be one future of work. It will be contextual with each country having to confront its own challenges, which have been largely shaped by its history, level of social and economic development, culture and demographics. Furthermore, globalisation, demographics, technology and climate change will impact on how policymakers and institutions negotiate the new state of play (Shallowe 2018).

In the new landscape of the future workforce the main engine of this digital era will be in increasing the rate of innovation, experimentation and collaboration and as implied above it will be talented humans that will make the difference, not technology. New technologies will impact how knowledge is organised, distributed and completed and it is human talent that will need to adapt to the new landscape (The Economist Intelligence Unit 2016) for prospering. This means that attracting and managing talent will be different to how it has been conducted in the past.

In 2015, key findings from a survey conducted on 420 US and European (The Economist Intelligence Unit 2016) executives in sectors across several business functions and four industries: banking and financial services; healthcare; retail; and manufacturing [but not education] found that there is a clear imperative for organisations to add to digital skills but that over 94% of those surveyed considered a moderate or severe digital skills gap was preventing their organisations from reaching a required digital future. This is set against a backdrop of a shortage of digital literate people. A key finding was that coinnovation initiatives around research and development or customer engagement, where talent clusters of entrepreneurial activity located together or across talent clusters offered "hot" digital technologies and capabilities, were speeding up innovation and impact.

Although there remains much that is unknown and still speculative it appears the case that knowledge work will be organised, distributed and performed in entirely new ways. A fusion of algorithms, automation, machine learning and the rise of new digital platforms is reinventing business models and changing how we see talent and how work gets done (The Economist Intelligence Unit 2016). This will have implications for the leading and managing of this talent.

There appears to be agreement that continuous learning is at the heart of maximising economic potential in the Fourth Industrial Revolution (Schwab 2016). Currently though, as the World Economic Forum (WEF) states:

> The skills required for most jobs are evolving rapidly but our adult education and training systems are lagging behind. While 35% of the skills demanded for jobs across industries will change by 2020, at least 1 in 4 workers in OECD countries is already reporting a skills mismatch with regards to the skills demanded by their current jobs. Thus, enabling and empowering workers to transform and update their skills is a key concern for businesses and societies across the globe.
>
> (WEF 2017)

The WEF's "An Agenda for Leaders to Shape the Future of Education, Gender and Work White Paper" report (2017), a multistakeholder dialogue group formed to accelerate global readiness for the digital workplace and realise the potential of human capital, sets out recommendations for a new learning strategy where sustained learning is core to thriving in the Fourth Industrial Revolution. Key strategies include:

- *Knowing what you've got – taking stock of existing skills* – currently there is no one comprehensive data collection organisation for adult skills although PIACC (OECD) and Digital Competency and Entrepreneurship Frameworks (EU) are authoritative and well recognised in the areas that they represent.
- *Evolution of a system to represent, understand and anticipate effective skills* aligned to labour market needs and the education system stakeholders at all levels.
- *Increased funding of resources for adult education*
  Funding should be made available for all adults but not focused on business and economic cycles. Seeking out different funding models and copartnership models with employers, or clusters of employers, to fund and scale up lifelong learning is required.This includes the adoption of personalised funding support for empowering individual learners, such as is already

implemented in France and Singapore. This would include publicly subsidised vouchers and individual learning accounts, tax deduction and preferential loans. However, sufficient time should be given by employers for staff development and learning. Initiatives should be complemented with more holistic and proactive approaches that effectively address motivation issues related to adult learning, as well as practical information and links to direct employment opportunities.
- *Targetting of specific sectors* – the SME's, older workers and lower-skilled workers.

Some areas will be more affected than others, where mechanisms and instruments are needed.

The WEF recommended strategy in the case of older workers is explored below.

Encouraging older workers' learning

> Helping older workers understand the range of training opportunities available to them (and encouraging their participation) is seen as crucial. Recent research in Italy highlights that older workforce members tend to underestimate the benefits of participating in training.
>
> Employers should consider dedicating more resources to training older workers, who tend to be more loyal employees and have considerable experience from which to draw upon in their upskilling efforts. Furthermore, governments can also help play a role in aligning these incentives. For instance, special funds and subsidies allocated to midcareer individuals above the age of 40, such as those in Singapore, can also help support the training efforts of older workers. As demographic shifts in many countries may result in a higher share of relatively older workers, employers and managers will need to better manage the needs of senior workers, work to cohesively integrate their intergenerational workforce and maximize opportunities for intergenerational learning and exchange.
>
> Source: World Economic Forum (2018:7).

Balancing out the winners and losers

The UK government sponsored independent review of working practices The Taylor Review (2017) considers the implications of new forms of work and who might be the winners and losers. It explores too, the implications for social justice and inclusion in the future of work and where all work in the UK economy should be fair and decent with realistic scope for development and fulfilment. It proposes that there is a need for a concerted approach to work which is both up to date, agile and based on enduring principles of fairness due to the pace of change in the modern economy, and particularly in technology and the development of new business models, where some could lose out. It calls for a laudable ambition for all work to be good work. The Review includes recommendations for specific measures in the short term as well as making the case for longer-term shifts.

What appears then in any discussion over the scenario for future workforces is recognising that it is critical that the productivity gains delivered through technology are more equal than unequal.

Global human capital trends

The annual Global Human Capital Trends report (2017) surveyed organisations, academics and practitioners around the world including 10,000 HR and business leaders across 140 countries. Findings show organisations are implementing models which adopt the "networked nature of today's world of work; innovation-based HR platforms; learning and career programmes driven by social and cognitive technologies; and employee experience strategies that put the workforce at the centre." This report considers the future of work driven by advances in automation and an expanded definition of the workforce. It identifies ten human capital trends among which the employee experience was key in all. Organisations are widening their focus to implement strategies that make the workforce central to include an employees' journey and experience from first contact to retirement and beyond, studying workforce needs, workplace redesign, well-being and work productivity systems.

The survey shows that what is meant by a career is rapidly changing forcing companies to adapt to readily available learning, personalised learning which allows an employee to build skills easily. New learning models are challenging the idea of traditional and static careers which are disappearing, and leading organisations surveyed are responding accordingly.

Source: The Global Human Capital Trends 2017, Deloitte.

The sociologist Richard Sennett in his book "The Culture of New Capitalism" (2006), exploring the diminution of social capitalism, writes of the spectre of uselessness as a result of global migration and automation and "where as Rifkin notes the realm of uselessness expands as machines do things of economic value of which human beings are incapable" (Sennett 2006:94). Ageing, Sennett comments, is viewed as a domain of uselessness fine-tuned to the economy when at some point as we all age, we become unproductive economically. Why is this so? Sennett's response is that it is sheer prejudice, where a cutting-edge innovation organisation tends to view older employers as slow, losing energy and unable to change and where middle-aged women are often stigmatised.

Set against the paradox of us all living longer and where health advances means most are healthy into their eighties there is a further ten or twenty years of productive giving after what has been the standard retirement age of sixty or sixty-five (now being pushed back in many countries) and where the spectre of uselessness could be kept at bay (ibid.).

Nevertheless, a limitation to paid work can be viewed as pernicious as it suggests that as a world we are only economically driven and if you are not involved in work that involves economic exchange, you are a burden for being unproductive. The debate needs widening out to include other work, such as volunteering or caring responsibilities by relatives in ageing economies. As referenced earlier, language too creates our notions of what are problems and what are the solutions to those problems. Governments will need to ensure that the digital economy is inclusive in workplaces and put into place policies that ensure all are included as part of a social justice agenda.

As Lund and Hazan (2018) emphasise, continuous learning is critical for business success in organisations of the future. The objective will be a learning environment adapted to a world of increased employee mobility rather than the more current siloed way of working. Lynda Gratton and Andrew Scott in their book "The 100 Year Life" (2016), based on their research, propose that living longer will result in significant changes and a rescoping of the traditional view of a working life of working from the ages of 21 to 65 and then having a retirement of some 30 years. It is now not affordable for the majority of people.

Living longer will, they say, result in substantial changes and a redesign of life. However, although we are living longer, most of us will need to work for longer with working lives extending into the 70s and 80s. At the same time, the traditional pattern of education, followed by a single continuous career and then retirement is under threat. Meeting the challenge of this change will necessitate lifelong learning as learning gained in your twenties, will not sustain you over the course of a 60-year career. Commensurately, the shape of a working life will take the form of certain times when there is a stronger emphasis and focus on work but at other times there is chance of an improved working live, possibly part-time with more flexibility around working patterns (ibid.).

A report proposes that interdisciplinary skills development is critical as they align with the organisational shift to networks of teams. Learning should encourage and even push people to move across jobs, which would have the benefit of increased mobility. Leading organisations are adopting these types of learning strategies to help employees adapt in what is termed intelligent assistance (Deloitte 2017).

A Deloitte article summarising research conducted with a global network of over 2, 200 subject matter experts, to research what possibilities the future of work could hold, reveals that living longer seems to be challenging traditional ideas about careers, retirement and work–life balance and these changes in mindset are starting to affect the way people work. Discussing the expansion of the productive years, which disappointingly the research limits to economic employment, emphasises the need for lifelong learning which has led to what is referred to as the new reality of lifelong reinvention Stockton et al (2018).

As multigenerational workforces become the norm, it means the strengths of each generation can be used. Here the research indicates the value of older workers might improve but as role models for work ethics and where older workers are seen to be of value for mentoring the younger generations' interpersonal and leadership skills. This however fails to recognise the implicit inherent potential of older workers if given sufficient opportunities to flourish.

The research suggests organisations that can harness seven new realities in the future of work will move ahead of the competition:

Exponential organisations – which capture a blend of organisational techniques that employ the right mix of exponential technologies, business models and, crucially, human talent.

The unleashed workforce – a workforce freed from constraints and boundaries which uses the talent of traditional full-time employees, joint ventures, contractors, freelancers, crowds and augmented through robots. They do not take a one-size-fits-all approach to the employee experience.

Lifelong reinvention – For individuals, development should be part and parcel of their career journey through both formal and informal training. Leaders should consider implementing flexible policies inclusive of workers of all ages. The role of the public policymakers would be to ensure the adoption of, and adherence to anti-discrimination and anti-ageism laws across industries and sectors.

Technology, talent, and transformation

This reality recognises the economic value of work that will be seen through the increased productivity of human–machine collaboration as it spreads more widely across workplaces, industries, the service industry and the public sector.

Labour saving costs

While it is considered that robots will not be taking over jobs, rather they will be augmenting jobs, so there is an enduring requirement for human skills for what robots currently cannot do. Governments should put into place incentives to adopt lifelong learning and skills and develop systems for support when jobs do disappear or are displaced due to new technology.

The ethics of work and society

A deeper and objective understanding of changing laws and employment regulations, especially as they relate to the freeing up of the workforce will be needed. There will be a need for governments to regulate to protect workers' rights.

The nimble enterprise

It is suggested that smaller agile organisations can equally survive and thrive with better brand identity, vision, expertise, international networks and intangible assets than larger ones.

Regulated innovation

Further regulation of the so called "gig economy" will be seen around the use of gig workers and robots and regulation will continue to evolve in a complex scenario.

Source: Adapted from Stockton, H., Filipova, M. and Monahan, K. (2018) Deloitte. www.deloitte.com/insights

What is clear and reinforced in Chapter 2 and in the WEF report (2017) is that insufficient skills development is taking place to address the exigencies of a digital future. The OECD (2015) report over one in four adults reported a mismatch between their current skills and the qualifications required for their jobs. This is a worrying figure as approximately 35% of the skills demanded for jobs across industries will change by 2020 (World Economic Forum 2017). The ILO (2014) too have pointed to a worrying mismatch of skills in Europe. So, as the World Economic Forum state, enabling and empowering workers to transform and update their skills is a key concern and imperative for businesses and societies (ibid.). The rate of skills obsolescence has speeded up across all sectors such as medicine, law, engineering, manufacturing, so that people will need to relearn their skills many times across a lifetime of working. This is also problematic for older workers, as it is more expensive to retrain a fifty year old than to hire a recent graduate. An older employee will have a higher salary grade and retraining comes at an expensive cost to employers and a younger person may have more time in the workplace for that reinvestment cost to be recouped in increased performance.

The Fourth Industrial Revolution is fundamentally changing the nature of work and the meaning of career making it imperative to constantly refresh one's skills. Increasingly, the organisation's role is viewed as creating the environment and systems to allow employees to constantly learn and relearn. The idea is that the explosion of free content means that the learning organisation should seamlessly integrate internal and external content into its platforms (Deloitte 2017). However, who exactly is responsible for an individual's learning forms part of a widespread and ongoing debate and discussion in differing countries (see RSA case study in Chapter 5), as well as the extent to which a government, wishing to drive economic growth overall, has a responsibility and holds the purse strings.

Research conducted in the US and the UK suggest that the so-called 21st-century skills will emphasise interpersonal skills, higher-order cognitive skills and systems skills. In line with the growing demand for social skills in the labour market suggested by Deming (2015) organisations look to align the workplace cultural context where digital technology and globalisation are taking place and reduce the costs of that coordination (Bakhshi et al. 2017:14).

In the US, future demand for skills include teaching, coordination and social perceptiveness, in addition to related knowledge such as psychology and anthropology. Also, higher order cognitive skills will be in demand, for example, originality, the ability to express ideas and ability to engage in active learning. The landscape for the UK is similar, where there will be a call for higher-order cognitive skills which Bakhshi et al. (2017) show would be for example, "skills related to system thinking – the ability to recognise, understand and act on interconnections and feedback loops in sociotechnical systems, such as judgement and decision-making, systems analysis and systems evaluation" also feature prominently (Bakhshi et al. 2017:14). Some sectors will thrive more than others. In the UK for instance, education, healthcare and wider public sector occupations are, with some confidence, predicted to see growth. These findings are consistent with population ageing and a greater appetite for lifelong learning (ibid.).

Towards open and flexible lifelong learning systems, UNESCO Institute for Lifelong Learning

Recognition and validation of knowledge and competencies acquired through multiple learning pathways are nonetheless part of a lifelong learning framework. Societal developments are reinvigorating the relevance of education that is lifelong and lifewide. The concept is not new, but it maintains its prominence as a means of systematising and organising learning in a comprehensive and equitable way. It places the empowerment of learners of all ages at centre stage. Given the challenges of technological and scientific development, and the exponential growth in information and knowledge that we have noted, lifelong learning is critically important to coping with new employment patterns and achieving the levels and types of competencies required by individuals and societies. The operationalisation of open and flexible lifelong learning systems depends on mechanisms for the recognition, validation and assessment of knowledge and competencies across educational and working spaces.

Source: Adapted from UNESCO Institute for Lifelong Learning (2010). Annual Report 2009.

The paradox of schooling and the workplace is at the centre of a tension shown in the overall direction that compulsory education at primary and secondary school education in a neo-liberal environment, widely adopted by governments across many countries in their education policy making. The influence of the results of the global rankings of education systems through the Programme for International Student Assessment (PISA) a tri-yearly international survey, operated by the OECD which aims to evaluate education systems worldwide by testing the skills and knowledge of 15-year-old students is accelerating a drive to increasing accountability and a narrowing focus on core subjects. As Coates (2018) points out we can generate courses to support learners to achieve short-term objectives of passing examinations based on a limited curriculum or advance a type of school leadership that conceptualises a new or reframed leadership approach fit for technological advancement.

This drive for narrowness is in contrast to what a pipeline of what Bakhshi et al. (2017) consider that future workers will require; that of broad knowledge in addition to the more specialised features needed for specific occupations; "broad-based knowledge areas such as English language, history, philosophy and administration and management are all associated strongly with occupations projected to see a rise in workforce share" (ibid:14).

It is also a contradiction when future estimated skills needed will be in problem-solving, leadership, emotional intelligence, empathy and creative skills (PwC 2018).

Rethinking education – reconsidering the link between education and the fast-changing world of work, UNESCO

> A number of responses have been proposed to address the disconnection between formal education and training and the world of work, including retraining of workers, second chance programmes and stronger partnerships with industry. We have also noted a greater focus on career-adaptive competencies. Indeed, the quickening pace of technological and scientific development is making it increasingly difficult to forecast the emergence of new professions and associated skill needs. This has spurred efforts to establish more responsive education and professional skills development that include greater diversification and flexibility, allowing for the adaptation of competencies to rapidly changing needs. It implies ensuring that individuals are more resilient and can develop and apply career adaptive competencies most effectively. These competencies often include more emphasis on what have been variably termed "transferable skills," "21st-century skills," and "non-cognitive skills," including communication, digital literacy, problem-solving, team work and entrepreneurship. Relevant competencies are also developed

through self-learning, peer-learning, work-based learning (including internships and apprenticeships), on-the-job training, or through other experiences of learning and skills development beyond formal education and training. We must therefore envisage new approaches to education and skills development that capitalise on the full potential of all learning settings.

Source: Adapted from Rethinking Education and Skills for Inclusive and Sustainable Development Beyond. Thematic Think Piece for the UN Task Team on the Post-2015 International Development Agenda. Paris, UNESCO (2015).

Evaluating the risk to jobs

There is ongoing debate about the scale of jobs at risk to new technologies with different studies estimating different rates. Frey and Osborne's 2013 research on the risk to jobs from computerisation and technology in the US, weighting 700 occupational types, argues that 47% of total jobs are at high risk of disappearing over the next twenty years. The findings predict that computerisation will mainly be connected to low-skills and low-wage jobs. Rather than being replaced, low-skills workers will move to jobs requiring creative and social intelligence, but they will require additional and social skills (Frey and Osborne 2013). In the UK, the RSA have estimated that there will be a loss of 35% of jobs (RSA 2017).

A further study from the OECD conducted on automation, skills use and training building on the expert assessment carried out by Frey and Osborne in 2013, estimates the risk of automation for individual jobs for the 32 OECD countries that participated in the Survey of Adult Skills (PIAAC 2013). This research considered the share of jobs likely to be significantly disrupted by the automation of production and services and the characteristics of these jobs and that of the workers who hold them. The risk is also assessed against the use of ICT at work and the role of training in helping workers move across to new career opportunities (Nedelkoska and Quintini 2018).

Across the 32 countries included, almost one in two jobs are likely to be significantly affected by automation, based on the tasks they involve. With 4% of jobs in OECD countries participating in PIAAC being highly automatable (a probability of automation of over 70%) being the equivalent to more than 66 million workers in the 32 countries. A further 32% of jobs carry a risk of between 50 and 70% meaning that there is a possibility that a significant share of tasks could be automated, which changes the skills requirements of the roles (ibid.).

Overall, job roles in the Anglo-Saxon, Nordic countries and the Netherlands will be less subject to automation than those in Eastern Europe, Germany, Chile and Japan. Most importantly, the risk to automation is not distributed equally across workers and is focused around basic to low levels of education. Whereas, the least automatable occupations almost all require professional training or tertiary education. This research suggests a reduction in the risk to automation commensurate with educational attainment and skills sets.

Interestingly, further unequal distribution is seen in that the risk of automation is U-shaped, but the risk is even more pronounced for younger workers than for older workers. Furthermore, worryingly, workers in highly automatable jobs are three times less likely to participate in work-related training than those less at risk. Also, there is much less participation in formal training and/or distance learning outside the jobs which are considered most at risk. The findings calls for much more facilitation of work-related training and development for those who will be most affected (ibid.).

In a further study "Skills Matter: Further Results from the Survey of Adult Skills" (OECD 2016), based on selected countries from the same 2013 PIACC research indicates that older adults' proficiency in literacy is lower than those aged 25–34, but varies according to other aspects such as educational attainment. Across the selected OECD countries, skills most used at work are writing, problem-solving and reading while ICT and numeracy skills are least used. However, one in four adults have no or limited use of computers and one in two adults are proficient only in low levels of problem-solving in technology situations.

It needs to be borne in mind though that the PIACC analyses a limited amount of work skills and different mixes of skills are needed for different work tasks. Some skills will be of primary importance and for some tasks they will be used in conjunction with other types of skills in the form of common sense, expert reasoning, vision, physical movement, or social interaction so the landscape of what skills will be required is by no means complete. However, this study clearly states:

> Skills have become the global currency of 21st-century economies but this "currency" can depreciate as the requirement of the labour markets evolve and individuals lose the skills they do not use. To ensure that people acquire the right skills and that economies and societies make good use of those skills, a concerted effort is needed by governments which design financial incentives and favourable tax policies that are conducive to skills development; offer vocational training; employers who invest in learning and can motivate workers to put more of their skills to use; labour unions, which ensure that investments in training result in better quality jobs and higher salaries; and individuals, who take advantage of learning opportunities and deploy their skills at work and in everyday life.
>
> (OECD 2016:18)

However, it is not just skills training alone that is needed, compulsory education "needs to be got right" (Schleicher 2016), emphasising the role of educational policy and education leadership in developing young people with the right skills for the workplace.

The challenge for leadership of learning and development in future workforces

The fundamental question in thinking about the role of leadership in workplaces is to continue to inspire, motivate and improve the performance of employees by way of how career models should evolve to encourage continuous learning, improve mobility and nurture a growth mindset (Dweck 2017), in each employee on a sustained basis. For it is organisations that can get to grips with this challenge that will outperform their peers and competitors (Stockton et al. 2018). For business and HR leaders, the new models of working are a wake-up call to adapt or risk falling behind in hiring, employee engagement, productivity and product innovation (Deloitte 2017).

> Organisational leaders should brace themselves for potential rapid disruption caused by technological advances that could require substantial talent restructuring. Individual workers should seek to identify and target employment opportunities in areas where the demand for human workers is likely to increase, while also understanding and learning technology skills for sustainable employability.
>
> (Agarwal et al. 2018:10)

A transformation to a digitally led model also means digital reorganisation, suggesting more fluid, connected organisations. There is little that is new about this call for organisational structures to be more finely tuned to better reflect turbulence and change and where silo working remains stubbornly resolute, hampering knowledge flows. It does however suggest that there is an immediacy for new organisational models to replace old power structures and where it is suggested that "many companies are starting to junk old, rigid organisational models and are building the way for small, nimbler clusters of talent that serve a particular market or niche" (The Economist Intelligence Unit 2016:5) placing talent at the central core.

In doing so, this makes the move to mainstreaming a model following the early adopters of agile organisational models such as the digital giants Apple, Google and Facebook. Emphasising the imperative, The Economist Intelligence Unit (2013) findings support an argument for a speeding up the process:

> Our study reveals a clear imperative for leaders to build a roster of digital skill to accelerate innovation. These digital capabilities can help a company move from recognising that "something needs to happen" to "making something happen.
>
> Compared with more nimble and collaboration-orientated competitors, the metabolism for cycling ideas and innovations must increase to survive – companies need to develop flatter corporate structures, smarter governance and rapid decision-making, freeing them up to cycle faster than they have before."
>
> (2013:10)

Methods and structures to implement the transformation to the digital age are sketchy but Kauffman (2008) writing on complexity suggests living systems, and that includes workplaces, operate along a continuum of order and disorder. But there needs careful adjustment in tackling the speed at which transformations will accelerate. Adapt too slowly and there is a risk in being outgunned by competitors and failure to meet customer expectations, adapt too fast and the balance of an organisation and its culture can be disturbed. And, as with any change, it is how change is communicated that can make the difference.

Managing across generations will also feature as a key leadership challenge in multigenerational workplaces and there will be a key role in embracing diversity and inclusive workforces.

Realising true workplace diversity requires strong, leadership and managerial responses. Diversity is starting to take a central stage in organisations and will require sophisticated strategies. However, it is not merely a question around human resource strategies adapting to increasing complexity, it is about a vision for what an inclusive, responsive, innovative workspace should look like in future workplaces, which are a credit to themselves and their employees in open and inclusive societies. It is about asking how do workforces themselves see workplace diversity?

As the Society for Human Resource Development (SRHM 2015) report notes diversity policies are already embedded along gender, generational and ethnic lines and in companies' working arrangements with employees. Longer life spans will result in employees staying in the workplace until a later age. A large feature of future workforces will be the increase in diverse workforces as the volume of women entering the workplace augments, many of whom will be temporary or part-time workers and many working remotely. Diversity means encompassing all and will necessitate a multilayered, carefully thought out, managerial approach as companies strive to get the most out of their people in a highly competitive environment (ibid.). Hofstede's model on culture (1980) identified basic differences between national cultures. His research identified six dimensions: power distance, uncertainty avoidance, individualism – collectivism, masculinity – femininity and indulgence-restraint. These were later extended by a further dimension, long-term versus short-term orientation (Hofstede 2001). Although critics argue that the data based on IBM employees researched in subsidiaries in the 1970's are outdated and obsolete, as a paradigm the model can still help us understand the changes that are occurring as workforces become ever more globalised and diverse as the studies correlating the old country scores with related variables available on a year-by-year basis in many cases find no weakening of the correlations (Hofstede 2011). Although accepted that technological advancement does change culture, it is not considered that technological changes nullify the other dimensions (ibid.) and societies will not necessarily become similar.

Enabling and empowering workers to transform and update their skills is a key concern and imperative for businesses and societies, according to the 2017

WEF report. The technological advancements of the Fourth Industrial Revolution will make it possible to achieve higher levels of productivity and implement the Sustainable Development Goals (Dodds et al. 2016; ILO 2016). Thus, it will be important to equip people to stay ahead of technological change. To prepare the workforce for tomorrow, the attention has to be placed on educational, training and reskilling programmes (Bianco 2014).

How then can older cohorts of workers be best supported to remain and sustain their learning in the new way of working when half of their life skills will become obsolete in the second half of their lives (Deloitte 2017). We already know that older persons are less likely to engage in training if they cannot see the advantage and value of it. And furthermore, research has shown that they are not necessarily consulted on what it is they need. What people want to learn in work will vary widely.

In the same way that we do not entirely know what the world of work will look like in 2050, we also cannot be precise in what older careerists will require in terms of skills, learning and experiences. However, this chapter has posited some research informed notions of how to best harness their skills to ensure that older workers know that they are valued and can flourish.

As the independent UK government commissioned report the Taylor Review (2017) states "yet, as the labour market changes and industries come and go, the importance of lifelong learning is growing" (2017:14).

Adopting holistic support and working conditions for well-being in ageing workplaces – challenges and solutions

With an increase in older workers a more holistic view of managing human capital for inclusive workplaces will be required. It is possible to imagine that older workers will increase their stock and be seen as valued in workplaces and as significant assets. Nevertheless, it is impossible to escape the biological fact that even with increased longevity as humans, older workers will have to face some grave health challenges while still working. This then leads us to ask what can be done to mitigate and sustain the longevity of retention and long tail of an older cohort of workers increasingly necessary to meet labour demand.

A holistic support structure and the provision that it will entail should be seen as part of central corporate social responsibility for organisations and fits into a wider social justice agenda, which could be driven by public policy-makers and governments. As the ILO advise:

> There is the potential to monitor and improve the working conditions of workers in many sectors with the aim of reducing the probability that older workers in these sectors will exit the labour market due to work-related physical and mental health issues or poor work–life balance.
>
> (2018:48)

At both individual and societal levels work is linked with improved health and well-being where work provides a sense of purpose. Research consistently links work with improved physical, emotional and cognitive health, financial stability and security, and quality of life (US Senate Special Committee on Aging 2017:4).

Well-being can be seen as forming part of what is viewed as Decent Work. The International Labour Organization (ILO) is the United Nations world authority on the world of work and is concerned with social justice in the workplace. Its 2008 Decent Work Agenda is based on four pillars; that of employment creation, social protection, rights at work and social dialogue. There has been an increased urgency among international policy-makers, particularly in the wake of the global financial and economic crisis of 2008, to deliver quality jobs along with social protection and respect for rights at work to achieve sustainable, inclusive economic growth and eliminate poverty.

The beneficial effect of work at an older age. International Labour Organization

> For older persons, decent work means the opportunity to remain an active part of the economy and society in conditions of dignity, freedom, equity and security. This, in turn, calls for the promotion of their working capacity, to allow them to adapt to changing demands and opportunities in the working environment. Since as early as 1930, the ILO has emphasised the need for special efforts to protect the jobs of older workers.
>
> Source: International Labour Organization. (n.d.) www.ilo.org/global/topics/decent-work/lang–en/index.htm

Decent work and the sustainable development goals

During the UN General Assembly in September 2015, decent work and the four pillars of the Decent Work Agenda became integral elements of the 2030 Agenda for Sustainable Development. Goal 8 of the 2030 Agenda (UN 2015) calls for the promotion of sustained, inclusive and sustainable economic growth, full and productive employment and decent work and the key aspects of decent work are widely embedded in the targets of many of the other 16 goals of the UN's development vision. This commitment and associated action plans stretch across the G20, G7, EU, African Union and other multilateral and regional bodies to recognise the significance of decent work to crisis recovery and sustainable development.

Decent work for older persons in Thailand, International Labour Organization

This case study focuses on a developing country facing policy challenges in coping with the impact of rapid population ageing of the labour market, and thus on the country's productivity and socio-economic development. The case presents insights that are also relevant for many other countries which share a similar socio-economic, demographic and politico-institutional setting.

The newness of the issue of decent work for older persons in Thailand offers an opportunity to engage government agencies at national and local levels, employers' organisations and workers' unions, CSOs, research institutions and community groups from the early stages of policy formulation. This allows for their various interests to be reflected in the relevant policies and potential activities to supplement each other. In this undertaking, Thailand can learn from other countries in the region that have experienced population ageing and devised measures to deal with the challenges to the labour market.

Creation of employment opportunities for older persons and upgrading of their income generating potential needs to be promoted in tandem with skill enhancement among older persons who want to work, in such a way as to respond to the changing needs of the labour market. For this purpose, expansion of currently limited lifelong learning opportunities would be useful for present and future older persons.

In a rapidly ageing society like Thailand, the promotion of employment opportunities for older persons is timely and indispensable for enhancing the country's productivity and socio-economic development, as well as the sustainability of social security schemes. Flexible retirement is an option to be explored, particularly in the public sector. Raising awareness of the potential of older workers in the private sector is also essential, with the collaboration of employers' organisations and workers' unions. Government provision of incentives, such as subsidies for measures in favour of retaining and re-employing older persons may be useful. Meanwhile, the promotion of employment opportunities needs to be pursued as an option, and not an obligation for older persons, taking into account their skills and needs.

Promoting decent work for older persons thus needs to be addressed as a society-wide and intergenerational issue. Raising the minimum wage for the working age population can contribute to greater savings into older age. Enhancing skills of the younger age groups can provide a basis for them to upgrade their skills when becoming older. The participation of the working age population in social security schemes not only enhances their security as they age but it also contributes to the sustainability of the country's social security system.

Source: Adapted from R Fujioka, F., and Thangphet, S. (2009) Decent work for older persons in Thailand. ILO Regional Office for Asia and the Pacific. Bangkok: ILO, (ILO Asia-Pacific working paper series) Asian Decent Work Decade.

As the Taylor Review (2017) emphasises:

> The shape and content of work and individual health and well-being are strongly related. 'For the benefit for firms, workers and the public interest we need to develop a more proactive approach to workplace health' (p. 9). With more and more people working well into their sixties, many individuals will now spend around 50 years of their life in paid work. As such, work is strongly related to the quality of individuals' lives and their well-being. Quality jobs increase participation rates, productivity and economic performance, whereas, low-quality work can push people out of the labour market or in to work which does not fully utilise their skills and experience, reducing well-being and productivity.
>
> (Taylor Review 2017:11)

Furthermore, the same review (2017) accentuates that:

> In an ageing workforce, more people will be affected by temporary or intermittent health conditions or time-limited caring responsibilities. It makes strong social and economic sense to make sure they are able to stay in rewarding and fulfilling work.
>
> (Taylor Review 2017:11)

It makes several recommendations from the National Institute for Health and Clinical Excellence (NICE 2015) guidance on organisational commitment to make health and well-being a core priority for top management in the NHS, the UK's national health service and the largest employer in Europe, which is highly relevant to other sectors and situations. The guidance places a clear focus on the strategic importance and benefits of healthy workplaces, encouraging a consistent, positive approach for all. The guidance is clear that top managers and leaders with remit for workplace health should address the issues of:

- physical work environment;
- mental well-being at work;

- fairness, justice, participation and trust;
- senior leadership;
- line managers' role, leadership style and training;
- job design.

An update to the same guidance, also includes guidance on older workforces. Management should also recognise transitions that "people are driven by different motivations at different points in their career and so what represents quality to them now may not represent quality ten years later" (Taylor Review 2017:10). This aligns with the research findings of the higher education case study outlined in Chapter 3 where different motivations are seen at different points of the working life cycle. Maintaining a skilled and healthy workforce is central to organisations as many societies age and well-being at work, working conditions and a good work–life balance will be core. Companies will be obliged to make adaptations, and some are already doing this to reflect transitions.

A set of examples follows where health and well-being are considered for older workplaces and where adaptation can take place.

Adapting workplaces to suit individual older worker needs. ŠKODA, vehicle manufacture, Czech Republic

As part of its commitment to its workforce under its corporate social responsibility initiative, Škoda guarantees that all workers who have been with the company for more than 30 years, in a case where they can no longer fully perform their role due to health issues, that their workplace will be adapted to meet their requirements or (where possible) they will be redeployed to a different job within the company. For a certain number, so called "protected workplaces" are available offering an adjusted working environment to meet their needs. Together with the company's wider commitment to improve health and safety and health promotion, these measures are designed to allow employees to extend their working lives up to retirement. Other measures include a fourteen-day recondition/curative stay at selected and preventative rehabilitation programmes, in order to lower risks of absenteeism and ensure seniors maintain a good standard of health.

Source: Adapted from *Employers' Practices for Active Ageing* (2012). Final synthesis paper of the European Employers' Organisations project on age management policies in enterprises in Europe.

The Alexander technique – using holistic support to avoid pain and injury

One approach to avoiding pain or injury at work and reducing absenteeism is the Alexander Technique (AT). This self-help method has been the subject of scientific trials and has been recommended for National Health Service funding. It is a form of skill-based coaching with therapeutic effects and aims to help people respect the design and function of the body.

Traditionally – whether using a screen, involved in manual handling, or bending over a specialised task – employees have no sense of whether their body is being used safely and no practical understanding of the risks involved. The need for better understanding arises only when things go wrong – chronic pain sets in and does not respond permanently to more common musculoskeletal interventions such as physiotherapy, osteopathy etc. Younger people can get away with recurrent abuse of the body, but if no guidance is given, the chickens will come home to roost in later life, interfering with productivity and everyday living.

AT coaching is most effective when delivered in one-to-one sessions over several weeks. Working on the individual's neck, shoulders or back the tutor gently adjusts muscle behaviour, visits the employee on site or asks them to demonstrate the demands of the job, and devises a less risky way to carry it out. Guidance will vary slightly – but critically – from person to person, which is why one-to-one sessions work best.

Once the employee has learned the skills involved they can apply them mindfully to any task, with little extra tuition needed. And also, to performing better with, say, golf or at the gym. A secondary benefit of the Alexander Technique is its power to combat stress and related disorders such as headaches, digestive problems etc. Once someone has learned to identify early warning signs they can destress within minutes.

Case study: Mr S, 56, had several sessions for shoulder pain. It transpired that the arms of a new office chair were preventing him from operating his keyboard and screen at a distance appropriate to his build. The chair arms were removed, and as his shoulder pain abated he also found a) that his asthma attacks reduced and b) he felt better able to manage his fear of flying. He said he felt much more aware of the early warning alerts and was now able to stop things in their tracks or manage them better. Colleagues and friends noticed that as the pain diminished his posture improved and he appeared younger.

These three apparently unrelated issues were interlinked through the Alexandrian discovery of neuro-muscular "primary control."

The system can also be applied to learning. In later life the prospect of adapting to new tasks can be daunting and stressful. A tense state of mind naturally diminishes one's ability to learn, and the Alexander Technique can be a calming and productive experience. The changes produce better energy levels – thereby aiding the learning process. The skills can also be applied to problem-solving and decision-making. For an employee to take a few minutes out – releasing areas of muscle tension, halting over-use of the body, improving the quality of breathing and clearing the brain – results in proven benefits for the employer.

Anna Cooper, Senior Practitioner, Alexander Technique, Society of Teachers of the Alexander Technique, https://alexandertechnique.co.uk/

The next chapter sets out the issues for learning and development of older workers seen in other contexts.

References

Agarwal, D., Bersin, J., Lahiri, G., Schwartz, J., and Volini, E. (2018). *The Longevity Dividend: Work in an Era of 100-year Lives*, 2018 Global Human Capital Trends. www2.deloitte.com/insights/us/en/focus/human-capital-trends/2018/advantages-implications-of-aging-workforce.html [Accessed 17/8/2018].

Bakhshi, H., Downing, J., Osborne, M., and Schneider, P. (2017). *The Future of Skills: Employment in 2030*. London: Pearson and Nesta.

Bianco, A. (2014). 'The job quality in the 21st century: a road map to a new development model'. *Quality Issues and Insights in the 21st Century, 3(1)*, ISSN 2029-9575.

Coates, M. (2018). *Take Me to Your Leader*. Unpublished Article.

Deloitte. (2017). *The Global Human Capital Trends 2017*. Deloitte. https://www2.deloitte.com/uk/en/pages/human-capital/articles/introduction-human-capital-trends.html [Accessed 2/12/2018].

Deming, D. (2015). *The Growing Importance of Social Skills in the Labor Market*. Tech. Rep. 21473, NBER Working Paper. Cambridge, MA.

Dodds, F., Donoghue, D., and Roesch, J.L. (2016). *Negotiating the Sustainable Development Goals: A Transformational Agenda for an Insecure World*. London: Routledge.

Dweck, C. (2017). *Mindset*. London: Robinson.

The Economist Intelligence Unit. (2013). *The Workforce of the Future Index*. London: Economist Intelligence Unit.

The Economist Intelligence Unit. (2016). *The Future of Work*. London: Economist Intelligence Unit in partnership with Cognizant.

European Employers Organisations. (2012). *Employers' Practices for Active Ageing*. Final synthesis paper of the European Employers' organisations project on age management policies in enterprises in Europe Published December 2012. London: European Employers Organisations.

Frey, C.B., and Osborne, M.A. (2013). *The Future of Employment: How Susceptible Are Jobs to Computerisation?* Oxford Martin School (OMS) working paper. www.oxfordmartin.ox.ac.uk/downloads/academic/The_Future_of_Employment.pdf [Accessed 27/7/2018].

Fujioka, R., and Thangphet, S. (2009). *Decent Work for Older Persons in Thailand*. ILO Regional Office for Asia and the Pacific. Bangkok: ILO, ILO Asia-Pacific working paper series, Asian Decent Work Decade.

Gratton, L., and Scott, A. (2016). *The 100 Year Life*. London: Bloomsbury.

Hofstede, G. (1980). *Culture's Consequences: International Differences in Work-Related Values*. Beverly Hills, CA: Sage.

Hofstede, G. (2001). *Culture's Consequences: Comparing Values, Behaviors, Institutions and Organizations across Nations*. Thousand Oaks, CA: Sage (co-published in the PRC as Vol. 10 in the Shanghai Foreign Language Education Press *SFLEP Intercultural Communication Reference Series*, 2008).

Hofstede, G. (2011). 'Dimensionalizing cultures: the Hofstede model in context'. *Online Readings in Psychology and Culture, 2(1)*. doi:10.9707/2307-0919.1014

ILO. (2014). *Skills Mismatch in Europe*. Geneva: International Labour Organization. www.ilo.org [Accessed 27/7/2018].

ILO. (2016). *World Employment and Social Outlook: Trends 2016*. Geneva: www.ilo.org [Accessed 27/7/2018].

ILO. (2018). *World Employment Social Outlook: Trends 2018* [Summary]. Geneva: International Labour Organization. www.ilo.org/global/research/global-reports/weso/2018/WCMS_615672/lang–en/index.htm [Accessed 27/7/2018].

ILO, BIAC. (2010). *A Skilled Workforce for Strong, Sustainable and Balanced Growth: A G20 Training Strategy*, Business and Industry Advisory Committee to the OECD (BIAC). Geneva: International Labour Organization.

International Labour Organization (ILO). Decent Work (n.d.) https://www.ilo.org/global/topics/decent-work/lang--en/index.htm [Accessed on 12/12/2018].

International Labour Organization. (n.d.). www.ilo.org/global/topics/decent-work/lang–en/index.htm [Accessed 18/8/2018].

International Organisation of Employers (IOE, BIAC). (2010). *Lifelong Learning Strategy – G20 Meeting*. Business and Industry Advisory Committee to the OECD (BIAC). Geneva: ILO.

Kauffman, S. (2008). *Reinventing the Sacred*. New York: Basic Books.

Lund, S., and Hazan, E. (2018). *Work in an Age of Automation*. Project Syndicate. www.project-syndicate.org/commentary/automation-ai-future-of-work-skills-by-susan-lund-and-eric-hazan-2018-07 [Accessed 31/8/2018].

National Institute for Health and Care Excellence (NICE). (2015). *Workplace Health: Management Practices*. NICE guideline [NG13] www.nice.org.uk/guidance/ng13/chapter/recommendations [Accessed 14/7/2018].

Nedelkoska, L., and Quintini, G. (2018). *Automation, Skills Use and Training*. OECD Social, Employment and Migration Working Papers, No. 202. Paris: OECD. doi:10.1787/2e2f4eea-en

OECD. (2013). *Skills Outlook 2013- First Results from the Survey of Adult Skills*. The Organization for Economic Cooperation and Development (OECD). http://www.oecd.org/skills/piaac/ [Accessed on 12/12/2018].

OECD. (2015). *Education at a Glance 2015*. Paris: OECD.

OECD. (2016). *Skills Matter: Further Results from the Survey of Adult Skills*, OECD Skills Studies. Paris: OECD. doi:10.1787/9789264258051-en

PwC. (2014). *The Future of Work – A Journey to 2022*. www.pwc.co.uk/services/human-resource-services/insights/the-future-of-work-a-journey-to-2022.html [Accessed 27/7/2018].

PwC. (2018). *Workforce of the Future – The Competing Forces Shaping 2030*. PriceWaterhouseCoopers. www.pwc.com/people [Accessed 20/8/2018].

Schleicher, A. (2016). *Why Skills Matter*. http://oecdeducationtoday.blogspot.com/2016/06/why-skills-matter.html [Accessed 18/8/2018].

Schwab, K. (2016). *The Fourth Industrial Revolution*. Colonia, Ginevra: World Economic Forum.

Sennett, R. (2006). *The Culture of New Capitalism*. New Haven and London: Yale University Press.

Shallowe, A. (2018). *Global Perspectives on the Future of Work*. Royal Society for the Arts (RSA). www.thersa.org/discover/publications-and-articles/rsa-blogs/2018/07/global-perspectives-on-the-future-of-work [Accessed 27/7/2018].

Skills for Employment. (n.d.). www.skillsforemployment.org/KSP/en/AboutThePlatform/index.htm#2

Society for Human Resource Management (SRHM). (2015). *Future Global Trends Affecting Your Organization – Engaging and Integrating a Global Workforce*. Society for Human Resource Management (SRHM) Foundation. http://futurehrtrends.eiu.com/report-2014/executive-summary/ [Accessed 18/7/2018].

Stockton, H., Filipova, M., and Monahan, K. (2018). *The Evolution of Work – New Realities Facing Today's Leaders*. Deloitte. www2.deloitte.com/insights/us/en/focus/technology-and-the-future-of-work/evolution-of-work-seven-new-realities.html [Accessed 16/7/2018].

Taylor, M. (2017). *Good Work: The Taylor Review of Modern Working Practices*. Tech. rep. London: Department for Business, Energy and Industrial Strategy.

UNESCO. (2010). *Annual Report 2009*. Hamburg: Institute for Lifelong Learning.

UNESCO. (2015). *Rethinking Education – Education and Skills for Inclusive and Sustainable Development Beyond*. Thematic Think Piece for the UN Task Team on the Post-2015 International Development Agenda. Paris: UNESCO.

United Nations. (2015). *Transforming Our World: The 2030 Agenda for Sustainable Development*. https://sustainabledevelopment.un.org/post2015/transformingourworld [Accessed 21/7/2018].

United States Senate. (2017). *A Report of the Special Committee on Aging*, Report 115-191. Washington: US Senate Special Committee on Aging, United States U.S. Government Publishing Office.

World Economic Forum. (2017). *White Paper Accelerating Workforce Reskilling for the Fourth Industrial Revolution – An Agenda for Leaders to Shape the Future of Education, Gender and Work*. www.weforum.org/whitepapers/accelerating-workforce-reskilling-for-the-fourth-industrial-revolution [Accessed 26/7/2018].

World Economic Forum. (2018). *The Future of Jobs Report, World Economic Forum*. Geneva. www.weforum.org. [Accessed 1/12/2018].

7 Exploring strategic implications

Chapter 7 explores wider strategic implications for major themes that have been raised through the case studies and empirical research in previous chapters.

This chapter is separated into three parts. Part 1 explores strategic implications for human resource management (HRM) at a macro level and Part 2 focuses on strategic implications for organisational learning and development at a meso level. Part 3 culminates in the drawing up of a theoretical model and theory of integration for sustainability and learning needs for older workers. This model is directly applicable to leadership and what strategic change and altered vision is required to best fulfil the potential of older workers.

PART 1: STRATEGIC IMPLICATION FOR HUMAN RESOURCES IN ORGANISATIONS AT A MACRO LEVEL

This book argues that diversity management should strategically move out of a more generally positioned domain of HRM to front line senior strategic organisational management. The aspects seen as important in managing and leading organisations relative to the role of older workers in the workplace are three-fold:

- managing equality and diversity in organisational policy
- work design for the older workforce and line management support
- addressing well-being for learning and its implications for older workplaces.

Managing equality and diversity in organisational policy

Notions of equality and diversity are enshrined in many government regulations and represent a social justice perspective, through the giving of equal opportunities. In the UK, for example, The Equality Act (2010) requires organisations to implement measures for fair treatment. The UK legislation covers sexual orientation, religion and age. In the higher education case study (Chapter 3 refers) the aspect of age was not considered by management (diversity implications and possible discrimination being omitted). Interestingly, inclusivity as part of the lexicon, was also absent, indicating age had not registered in management eyes as a diversity aspect and as a protected characteristic apart from recruitment and redundancy.

This was despite a strategic priority of an inclusive workplace focused on building a culture to provide opportunities for all to excel and advance. The organisation's stated values are that it aspires to be an exemplary employer where staff are valued and can see how they contribute to the whole. However, succession planning and a business imperative to inject new blood into an ageing organisation had resulted in a sense that opportunities were narrowing for older workers which raised a tension around the ideals for building and promoting an inclusive workplace.

It was thought that discrimination through ageism of professional staff was not overt but existed as in other organisations and society, relative to both genders, but was more pronounced for women as society suggests, aligned to research by McGann et al. (2016). Also, for this same study, although line management development covered responsibilities under The Equality Act (2010) it was striking that there were no staff development policies focused on older workers apart from retirement preparation. The annual Equality Data Report for this institution was underwhelming in relation to age with no specific and explicit mention as to affordances being given to age. Part of the necessary organisational shift to ensure potential is reached is in 'combating' discrimination of older workers. Perceptions of ageing and discrimination in the workplace is rife and perceptions of ageism in the UK, for example, are among the highest in Europe (Eurobarometer 2015). A recent British House of Commons paper has been sharply critical about the slow progress towards age equality opportunities (HoC 2018) in the UK tracing still existing and stubborn discrimination in employing older workers.

Managing diversity requires framing the debate as to whether learning and development at the later stages of a career is for a social justice or for a business objective with evidence indicating these aspects can be interdependent and mutually reinforcing as Arvinen-Muondo and Perkins (2013) suggest. Diversity policies strengthen organisational and human capital, which alongside knowledge capital, are principal intangible assets used by companies in a wide range of sectors to establish competitive advantage and create value (EU 2013).

Kirton and Greene (2005) present a case for diversity management centred around an equal opportunities discourse referring to practices accommodating workforces for diversity, whether based on geographical location, nationality, ethnicity, gender, religious affiliation, disability, age and other aspects of identity challenging discrimination that disadvantages people because of these aspects of difference. This "valuing differences" approach (as opposed to an assimilationist melting-pot approach or accepting-of-difference approach) reaches further than merely seeing an organisation as nondiscriminatory proposed by Arvinen-Muondo and Perkins (2013), and beyond what is legislated for, to one of being positively valued. It encompasses Sen's notion of flourishing (1993) "where harnessing these differences creates productive environments where all feel valued, where their talents are being fully utilised and in which organisational goals are met" (Kandola and Fullerton 2003:167). It is a proactive, strategically relevant and results-focused approach complementing equal opportunity initiatives recognising ethical and fair practice arguments can be combined with the recognition and valuing of difference as an opportunity to improve business performance (CIPD 2011).

Organisations establish modes of operating that can reflect unconscious assumptions and bias (Arvinen-Muondo and Perkins 2013). Diversity management includes ensuring talents are well used and staff retained. Part of this is in creating a culture supportive to difference when discriminatory attitudes and beliefs are a factor in older workers' job market withdrawal (EU 2012). Stereotypes and ageist assumptions including older people's learning capabilities in the vast majority have little credibility suggests Findsen (2015). However, some businesses have been reluctant to adopt a diversity approach through a critical human resource development strategy, as the empirical evidence is still evolving. But practically it is argued there is a strong business case for adopting it and which adds values (CIPD 2011).

Crucially, diversity and its acceptance is not just the responsibility of the organisation to create an enabling culture to diversity. Arvinen-Muondo and Perkins (2013) posit that it operates at an individual level, emphasising an active agentic role for older workers where the findings of the HE study showed there is a lack of empowerment. Understanding what organisations can do to promote diversity can be viewed at a macro level – the attitudes and characteristics of wider society in which the organisation is located, at a meso level – the organisation itself and at the micro level – attitudes and commitment of individual workers. Syed and Ozbilgin (2009) advance that different strategies are required at each level. The HE study largely focused on the meso and micro organisational levels.

Edwards (1987:45) suggests that reinforcing differences is not unproblematic when asking when is it more equitable to treat people differently because of their differences and when does different treatment become unfair discrimination corresponding with the unintended consequences of placing one group before another as Sen (1993) suggests. Regardless, good organisational practice means robust policies do not discriminate directly or indirectly, consciously or unconsciously for any protected characteristics. In practice, Arvinen-Muondo and Perkins (2013:30) consider good practice is often diminished by being narrowly focused on recruitment, training and promotion thwarting Sen's notion of flourishing and Kandola and Fullerton's (2003) characterisation of managing diversity where learning and development could play a positive role.

However, Arvinen-Muondo and Perkins (2013) propose a pragmatic business case for diversity management in that the argument for diversity is good for business and profitability, based on recruitment and retention of good staff, better services and products, better decision-making and a better reputation.

For the HE study, unions had recognised age as a protected characteristic but had largely not lobbied for its inclusion in the same way they had for gender and racism issues in HE. Furthermore, there was reticence seen by trade unions regarding age, which accords with Oosterwikj's (2015) findings over the reticence of unions in relation to age. A brief study of the major trade union websites in the UK, indicates that more emphasis appears to be placed on gender and ethnicity than for age.

To support this organisational shift, organisations that are adaptive to change have leaders who adopt adaptive leadership and management approaches which espouse complexity theory which take a great emphasis on learning, multiplicity, interaction and polyphony as a new approach to understanding the survival of organisations (Laitinen 2015). Some interesting research based on working with Generation X (under-40-years old) school leaders in London, New York and Toronto examined careers, leadership and future aspirations and shows that what older workers want in relation to development and organisational leadership collides in places with what millennials seek (Edge et al. 2017). The case study from Aviva in Chapter 5 also indicates convergence of some aspects between the two generations.

Work design for the older worker

It is clear from the research outlined in this book and the case studies in Chapter 5 that older workers should be supported in adapting to a changing workplace and emphasis needs to be placed on their appropriate work design and management to not only reap the best from them but to help support them so that they can realise their untapped potential. Some of this management will be in the form of line manager support for older workers.

UNESCO's report "Rethinking Education" states that "education is central to developing the capabilities required to expand the opportunities people need to lead meaningful lives in equal dignity" (2015:32) But the report also adds that "*the right to quality education is the right to meaningful and relevant learning*." This means that learning should reflect what each culture, each human group, defines as to what is required to live in dignity (2015:32) so ascertaining what each part of the workforce requires to have a fulfilling worklife needs to be understood, which would include hearing the voices of those so far unheard capturing the full diversity of workforces. A fundamental finding from the HE case study in Chapter 3 was that perceptions of older workers needed shifting to acknowledge development not dismissing those aged late 50s or 60s as career irrelevant or not having career goals. There is a gap in perceptions that some older workers may have a strong development perspective and not a maintenance one which appears to be a default model. However, older workers are not homogenous, and some will still look for an exit strategy as Kooij et al. (2008) research indicates.

The OECD (2006) "Agenda for Reform" to improve job prospects for older workers views employers as gatekeepers. It calls for a three-pronged approach: firstly, increased investment in lifelong learning at a midcareer point, secondly, following the requirements for adult learning, adapting teaching methods and content to older workers' needs, recognising prior learning and experience to increase attractiveness of training and potential returns. Thirdly, promoting later retirement itself encourages greater investment in training older workers as there is a better ROI through longer pay off times. Extended working lives means all need to continue to be motivated and supported (ibid.). Drawing on Habermasian spaces is vital, grounded in the HE study findings and through the literature so that older workers have the confidence (built into training) to discuss when certain things are blocking them which could be related to other people's perceptions of them as being old. Kanfer and Ackerman's (2004) research on age-related changes to motivation indicates focussing on intrinsic rewards around pay, promotion and recognition may not be as valued for this age group as these are often areas where older workers are constrained. Motivation for this grouping could be improved by adopting critical HRM age-related organisational strategies and managerial practices, advanced by Kooij et al. (2008) but further research into this area is needed as established motivation theory does not appear to apply.

The role of line management in supporting older workers

The seductiveness of age in remaining in the same groove and not extending new learning is suggestive of plateauing. McNair (2010) reports that employees and supervisors may conspire to underperform. Some plateauing appears related to organisational expectations in how staff might progress or in being given opportunities which negatively affect morale and performance. Line managers may find it more convenient to tolerate suboptimal performance than to train because costs and inconvenience of moving from "good enough" to maximum performance do not seem justified by potential gains or just allowing those to retire with dignity (ibid.). Factors associated with job content plateauing suggest employers need to ensure older workers with high-work centrality and learning self-efficacy are provided with challenging jobs fostering learning new skills. As important, is signalling to older workers they are valued and respected through HR practices targeted at older employees and respectful treatment from their supervisor and work group members is supported by Armstrong-Stassen (2008).

With no set retirement, there needs to be a way to ensure people are doing the job well. The suggestion of "mainstreaming" means that expectations of progression should be the "norm" as you would in a school, college or university environment. Why would workplaces be any different? McNair (2010) suggests that creating a sense of a positive future has a major influence on the work and training decisions of employers and employees. This places the responsibility to develop firmly on both the staff and organisations expectations when a finding from the HE study was that staff *wanted* the opportunity to rethink skills, how they used them and how they might improve them, emphasising agency. Empirical research and the case studies indicate a requirement and keenness to keep pace with development aligned to older workers continued motivation to participate in development. Findings in the HE research show that older workers also want to be given the opportunity to advance, underscored by the OECD (2013) survey of adult skills, where continuous development of skills to retain older workers' value in the workplace is needed.

The AAT report (2015) indicates low levels of technological skills are a barrier to reskilling and employability and there should be opportunities to extend learning to keep up.

In the HE research findings, wanting age-blind learning did not represent older workers' best interests. More suited to later career workers' interests would be tailored personal/professional development plans negotiated with line managers and reviewed at three-to-six monthly periods to revisit aims and objectives which is proposed by McNair (2011) and Altmann (2014). Mentoring, coaching and other development could offer valuable development.

Addressing well-being for learning and implications for older workplaces

Making the correlation of well-being to learning as Bingham and Bubb state is complicated:

> Although the link between well-being and learning and development is hard to establish directly, having good mental and physical health is a prerequisite to learning and acts as a barrier if absent.
>
> (Bingham and Bubb 2017:181)

Workplace stress can be mitigated by developing a supportive learning culture where learning creates positively valued outcomes (Huysman 1999).

Older workers experience widespread feelings of vulnerability around losing jobs and not being able to replace them, loss of status, losing potency in relation to men and women, health and loss of confidence. How older people are seen in society impact significantly on confidence levels (Bingham 2017), augmented by widespread constant restructuring and redundancies in many sectors and countries. This is particularly salient when research indicates that the unemployed 50+ age grouping are often unable to find another job (McNair 2011).

Perhaps the vulnerability factor is unsurprising as there is a strong association between the importance of work for people's personal needs in terms of meaning, role, status and social engagement as well as finance seen in McNair's findings (2010). Signals that employment is secure (and investment in training can be such a signal) bolsters confidence (ibid.). In the HE research staff and management reflected on older people's increasing humbleness as they aged. Older people feel less confident about some aspects of their lives, but more in others, indicating increased mastery in life. A question arises as to whether "humbleness" reflects badly on older workers leading them to be seen as "invisible" or "weak"? Although there was a strong sense of joint responsibility to develop in the HE study, some individuals wanted to be "sanctioned" by the organisation to give a sense of empowerment and encouragement. This finding threw up a potential tension between the desire for "self-promotion" and "self-worth" conjoined with a certain workplace vulnerability.

The evidence from findings on confidence change indicates a significant role for government policy and organisations in supporting and nurturing an older workforce as Bingham (2017) and Altmann (2014) recommends.

PART 2: ORGANISATIONAL IMPLEMENTATION AND PROCESS AT A MESO LEVEL

Part 2 focuses on strategic implications for organisational learning and development at a meso level for:

- managing key aspects of transitions
- addressing well-being for learning and implications for older workplaces
- knowledge sharing and intergenerational dialogue
- staff review and development as a performance tool.

Managing key aspects of transitions

There is a link between vulnerability and transitions which affect esteem and confidence. Not only society labels older workers, research showed pejorative language was used by older people to talk about themselves (Bingham 2017). The HE study indicates that management recognition of vulnerability in transitions should be aligned to an equity and diversity approach to people management and the necessity to build up inclusive workplace environments which policy recommends (European Commission European Employment Observatory Review 2012). Parity of esteem was considered lower for older administrative staff on lower grades (where a good proportion are female) highlighting the fine grain managing of diversity across different pay grades and seniority (Bingham 2017). However, there is a real danger in seeing differences as benign which overlooks the role of power, conflict, dominance and history of how organisations are fundamentally structured by race, gender and class (Johnson and Schwabenland 2013) and I argue, age. This aspect aligns to critical educational gerontology as a concept of praxis and action. Its purpose is "to prevent premature decline, to facilitate meaningful roles, encourage psychological growth and improve social attitudes towards ageing" (Findsen and Formosa 2011:54).

Older workers' perspectives are often one of *being in limbo* leading to an absence of valuing and closing down, rather than one of progressing (Bingham 2017). A demographic tipping point is being reached where ad hoc processes are insufficient. The ending of enforced retirement age (seen in an increasing number of countries) has resulted in uncertainties, as well as a lack of transparency over succession planning, due to a reticence to discuss approaching retirement by older workers (ibid.). Management of learning and development around transitions should be advanced for all workers and translated into formalised policies and procedures. Solutions could be in staff development personal development plans, in encouraging trust and transparency, in coaching and using the staff reviews to link to the career service. Line management is key to helping staff manage transitions (Boxall and Purcell 2008) and expert outplacement companies can support (see Chapter 5).

Responding to equity needs in transitions for development

In the HE study, management pointed to inadvertent discrimination around broader development in transitions and different life stages which was seen as inevitably affecting older women more than younger women or men. Staff concern about equal opportunities was reflected in a call for the benefits of having older workers reviewed. There was recognition of the lack of inclusivity in development by some management, with no clear pathways for staff not classed in the academic category, which raises questions of equity over differences and demarcation between the two job categories.

Mobility concerns stagnation, transparency around equity and how it could be improved for organisational strategic development and innovation to benefit older workers more widely. Effective development should be geared around the organisation but should also acknowledge the value for an individuals' progression either within the organisation, outside or in a person's personal life, aligned to learning theory which extends beyond the workplace, as supported by Hodkinson et al. (2004).

However, more generally older workers do not move on. Development for older workers should be seen as a tool for providing mobility out of the organisation for self-employment beneficial to being a dynamic organisation as Boxall and Purcell (2008) propose. Skilling those who want to move aids succession planning and is vital for organisations. Line management then play a crucial role in enabling or disabling opportunities for that progression (ibid.).

Organisational transparency in how and why roles are parcelled allow route maps to development across organisations. As Harteis and Goller (2014) point out, transparency and equity permits space for aspirations and route maps to development resulting in enhanced work agency helpful to older workers looking for more flexibility.

Older workers do not necessarily want career development in the same area. What alternative skills and knowledge would they require to change direction? Joyce and Showers (1980) suggest that starting with personalising learning, understanding older workers have more experience (but not necessarily the right kind) and potentially more learning, would open up the conversation. A needs assessment tool could result in new work opportunities with retraining. Development suggestions include coaching, refreshers, confidence boosters and revival skills tailored to older workers and shadowing which proactively encourages movement within the organisation as McNair suggests (2011). For those in the HE study, significantly types of development offered were not best fit and it was mentoring, coaching, workplace relationships, team working and partnerships being the uncosted, unfunded development that made the difference (coaching in this study was unfunded, reliant on volunteers).

Addressing well-being for learning and implications for older workplaces

Having a broader conception of what development for older workers is would help participation where it is often not at optimum take-up (McNair 2011) making it more relevant and an everyday occurrence and which offers a more expansive view of development as posited by Evans et al. (2002). This means formalising areas such as coaching and mentoring, including self-directed learning and networking through professional associations which all represent personal development. This type of development can be more valuable in later career stages. Formalising informal learning; making explicit how networking learning operates without excessively formalising it such as professional learning communities (Stoll et al. 2006) fits into this holistic view. It actively promotes internal mobility together with line management effectiveness to move beyond a box ticking formality and facilitate personal learning (Joyce and Showers 1980). The concept of the workplace as sites of learning requires overhauling in a time of changing demographics.

Knowledge sharing and intergenerational dialogue

Knowledge sharing when existing informally could be extended and explicitly formalised. While in the HE study the individualistic nature of the organisational culture hindered knowledge nonetheless, the desirability of collaborative working is supported by Findsen (2015) where through group participation both experienced and nonexperienced workers build collective knowledge as a community of learners and learning, advancing collective knowledge through modelling, coaching, mentoring and scaffolding which offers equal footing with younger workers (ibid.) and for which the findings of Osborne's large study also align in that expertise is no longer built in the competence of individual employees. Competence is based on network and organisations resolving working life problems together. Thus, organisations must be sufficiently flexible to be capable of networking (Osborne 2015).

However, there are concerns around knowledge sharing, relevant in times of organisational change and concerns over job security which raises the question of "value to whom"? Jarvis (2004) is critical in pointing out that power relations are absent in discussions around workplace learning where "learning organisations are not neutral places" and the reality is that who gets favourable treatment in workplace learning is directly related to the exercise of power relations in often complex circumstances, according to Findsen and Formosa (2011:40). Nevertheless, there is evidence of gaining value from and giving value to others in knowledge sharing through capitalising on older colleagues' knowledge, and the value placed on mentoring as forms of knowledge recycling. While there is ambiguity in employers' attitudes to older workers in that skills and knowledge can be regarded as obsolete, Tikkanen and Nyhan (2006:11) consider that they are also viewed as "loyal and reliable particularly by younger workers." Utilising skills and knowledge in different ways can bestow continued value on workers moving to the last five or ten years of a working career (ibid.), aligned with the HE findings research on intergenerational sharing and the value it brings.

It is debateable whether formalised approaches to facilitate communication between different groups for knowledge sharing should occur as the HE study indicated. Nevertheless, with four generations sharing today's workplaces there is value in mixed-age workplace communities through intergenerational and intragenerational dialogue. Barnett (2012) helpfully proposes that creating intergenerational spaces encourages a potential beneficial two-way flow of knowledge and experience. Little researched as a practice, with no guiding rationale or framework (Findsen and Formosa 2011) mixing age groups can be beneficial for innovation and reciprocity and Zachery (2000) considers that it challenges preconceptions. Intergenerational learning could extend lifelong learning through "shared meaningful activities" (Brown and Ohsako 2003:173). Practically, a business blueprint for building values in multigenerational workplaces suggests learning gaps can be overcome through addressing knowledge (K), skills (S), abilities and attitudes (A), (Rhoades and Shepherdson 2011), while using networks and collaborations can develop supportive learning environments.

Organisational theories, such as those seen in complexity theory hold a critical approach to traditional management ideas, which argue that people in organisations can be managed and led by formal authority and preset, proforma systems. In contemporary workplaces other set-ups can be seen which challenge traditional structures and processes. These can offer other ways to manage learning such as through collaborative spaces, where tacit and experiential learning can take place.

Staff review and development as a performance tool

Strategic organisational development strategy and planning for development to include older workers requires constant review to adapt to external and internal change as part of strategic planning. As part of this, any staff review and development process as a tool for achieving organisational goals needs adapting and reviewing to be more holistic it its approach recognising transitions, as indicated earlier, which would strengthen robust processes to better reflect older workers' requirements and capture their needs.

In the HE research a crucial finding was that adapting to a performance management and appraisal process and using the staff review and development review as a performance management tool was supported by managers and staff. A key management objective was to revise the review and reward frameworks to strengthen a performance culture but having to negotiate with professional associations and the unions in fighting charges against "rampant managerialism" meant this has not been advanced.

The impact of learning should feed into any organisational practice, giving clarity and transparency into how a staff review fits into strategic planning, building a culture that provides opportunities for all to excel and advance. Any human resource development (HRD) strategy should closely mirror an overall strategic plan in the type and range of development offered to support and fulfil organisational objectives.

In terms of processes, there should be a formal requirement for line managers to take the career development component seriously (which was not the case in the HE case study), so best practice for staff review in learning organisations could be followed which Boxall and Purcell (2008:200, 219) advance.

PART 3: DEVELOPING A THEORETICAL MODEL AND FRAMEWORK FOR OLDER WORKERS' LEARNING AND DEVELOPMENT

Silverman (2013) defines theory as "a set of concepts used to define or explain some phenomenon" consisting of plausible relationships produced among concepts and sets of concepts (Strauss and Corbin 1994:78). A theoretical model is shown in the five pillars model framework below (Figure 7.1). The model offers a new framing for valuing older workers under five themes of *valuing, refocusing, retaining, involving and dialogue and fora for all* representing a higher order analysis. The five overarching themes represent the theoretical and empirical field for older workers' learning and development.

Valuing older workers provides the roof which, as a classical Ancient Greece construct, represents humanity but has utility at its core. The classic Greek post-and-lintel system is made of columns with an architrave over the top. The solid columns supporting the roof indicate harmony with their surroundings, adapting to the environment. Sustainability is shown through Grecian architecture still in existence. At the base is the *buleuterion*, a utility gathering space for meetings and assembly of citizens for dialogue within the *agora* (Charytonowicz 2014). Flourishing is enacted through learning and development *within and beyond workplaces* valuing and utilising older workforces for sustainable organisations. While this figure could appear on the surface as similar to UNESCO-style representations, the diagram is based on Aristotelian notions of *eudaimonia* indicating flourishing drawing on Sen's capability theory and the creation of Habermasian spaces to encourage flourishing for dialogue and sharing. It is a continuous cycle of development. Responding to the construct, a recommended organisational culture, climate and structure is proposed to address the challenge of sustainable workforces in demographic change for best practice in getting the best from an older workforce including:

- Age as part of a diversity model
- Dialogue to promote inclusivity and empowerment

- Changing the culture to one recognising transitions
- Organisational model for developing older staff
- Perceptions of organisation and staff career progression and development
- Retention of older workers' policy and support
- Development of a learning organisation
- Holistic approaches for development, learning and well-being
- Model creating a strategic continuum for professional and personal development
- Professional learning communities and networked learning (aligned to knowledge sharing).

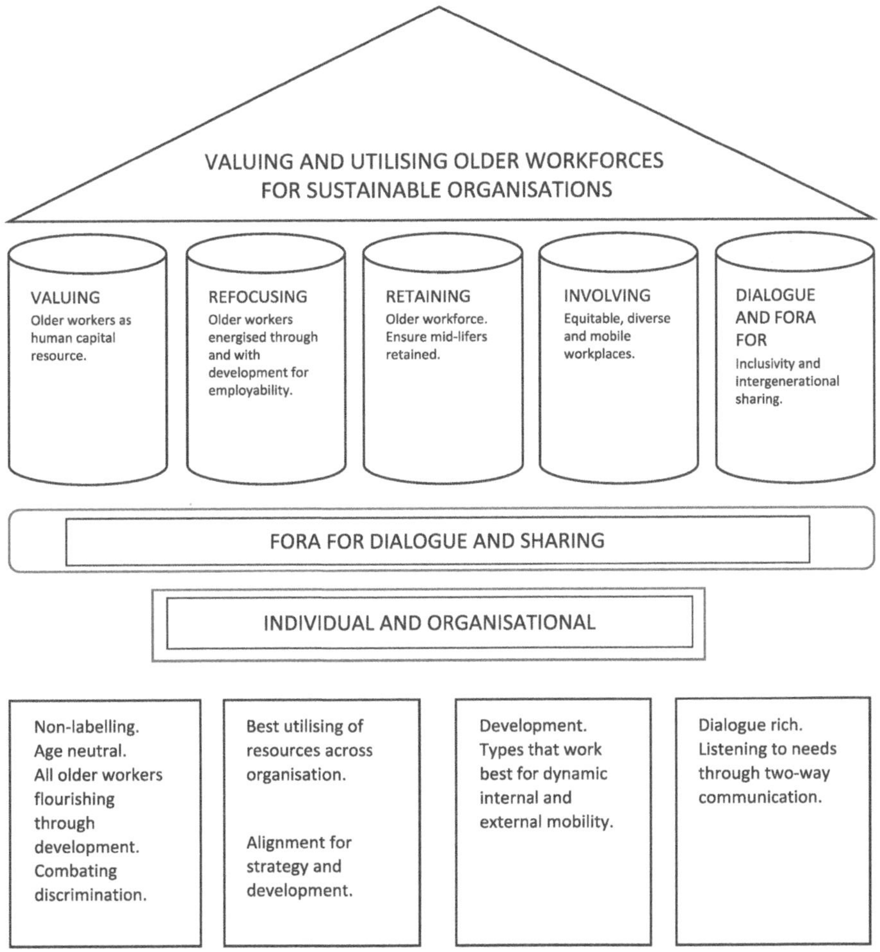

Fig 7.1 Valuing and utilising older workforces for sustainable organisations

I now turn to the revised conceptual framework shown in Figure 7.2 which is linked to Figure 7.1 in that it acts as an enabler by which the empirical field in Figure 7.1 can be enabled or facilitated. So, the value of the conceptual framework is seen through its operation and implementation as a lever to facilitate older workers' development through changed organisational structures and processes.

Proposing a revised conceptual framework

A conceptual scheme can help make sense of conflicting levels of phenomena in a "snapshot" in time embedded in an ongoing historical process having a relationship among and between them (Ritzer 2012).

This revised conceptual framework builds on the initial framework (Figure 7.1) reflecting development in thinking around older workers' development, acting as

Fig 7.2 Critical human resource development structure and processes for older workers' empowerment and flourishing through learning and development

an enabler for the theoretical and empirical field. It provides a bridge between the literature on socio-cultural and relationship theories of development aligned with theories of flourishing, work agency and empowerment through the creation of Habermasian spaces. This framework emphasises the HR aspect of Bolman and Deal's (2008) organisational frames in analysing organisational strategy which includes individual skills, needs, competency profiles, relationships, motivation levels, enthusiasm, harmony and cooperation.

The framework's major themes are; the importance of empowering older workers in their vulnerability and lack of confidence, the value seen in informal and tacit learning, the importance of increased spaces for dialogue in Habermas's ideal speech situations, recognition of transitions, a call for increased mobility and pathways for advancement, the value of knowledge sharing and intergenerational perspectives for mutual support and the role of enabling organisational climate and structures for supporting older workers in a more expansive form of development.

The key theories are in exercising capability (Sen 1993) and Habermasian dialogic spaces (Habermas 1984, 1987) shown in the centre as a twin device for transforming critical social change to work against the rationalised organisation for empowerment of older workers in development needs. To exercise both theories, the correct vectors need to be present through the overlapping enabling elements of the framework. The HR strategy is the overarching component shown in the outer rim in which all elements are nested indicating a strategic organisational role for HR. Each smaller element (vectors) relates to and enacts on the other in a dynamic environment for flourishing, moving some way towards a conceptual understanding of older workers' workplace learning.

The model accentuates an organisation's acknowledgement of the diversity of needs to support workplace learning cultures sympathetic to older workers and recognition of the need to align with more holistic understandings of workplace learning, supported by Tikkanen and Nyhan (2006). Sen and Habermas's respective theoretical frames are sensitive to notions of emancipation and agency having inferences for how learning is structured in organisations. Sen's framing requires enabling preconditions to be present while Habermas's approach requires dialogic communication legitimised in the workplace. Flourishing can help stimulate communication to develop positive institutional and departmental cultures. As Sen and Habermas's philosophical writings offer little insight into the practices of affordances, that is possibilities for action (Gibson 1979), these critical theoretical underpinnings demonstrate how the translation to hard processes, moving the discussion from theory to praxis, could occur (Terry 1997).

Social-cultural theories encompass an intersection of factors having the most relevance to contemporary workplace learning (Baumgartner 2001; Evans et al. 2002; Unwin 2009; Hager 2010). Drawing on work agency and organisational theories the framework conceptualises a new reciprocal and interdependent model suggesting a paradigm shift in organisational development to better reflect older workers' development needs but a model which is mutually beneficial to staff and management.

As discussed, the themes shown in the model contribute to the argument in proposing a bridge between existing theories of development, and aligning the theories of flourishing, agency, and empowerment for a critical organisational structure arguing for different requirements across the life course. The framework advances the study in older workers' learning proposing a framework of use to both the older workforce and management when there is no overall conceptual framework or model existing at organisational level in how to implement workplace practices of benefit to older workers and the organisation (Tikkanen and Nyhan 2006).

Critical theory "seeks to highlight, nurture and promote the potential of human consciousness to reflect critically upon such oppressive practices and thereby facilitate the extension of domains of autonomy and responsibility" (Alvesson and Wilmott 1996:13). This critical HR framework expands on the traditional literature considering social and demographic contexts of ageing workplaces. Traditionally, HRD literature has been based around functionalist and performativity perspectives with little attention paid to the wider social, economic and political contexts in which it operates (Elliott and Turnbull 2005).

This revised conceptual framing of older workers' development aligns with Barnett's (2012:3) multiplanar redesign for 21st-century workplaces, opening up spaces for intellectual collaborative thinking and imagining of possibilities where preconditions include an ethos of trust and "communicative openness" and where "something approaching a Habermasian ideal speech situation (ISS) is logically entailed where hierarchy and boundaries need to be temporarily set aside." Such a re-design supports having Sen's flourishing vectors *in situ* for flourishing to occur in all staff, including that of older workers.

The framework proposes a way forward for informed debate on establishing free speech situations without prejudice and fear of being labelled which when transformed into praxis permit a celebration of age similar to existing LBGT or BME groupings in this context. It aligns with Sen's capability in being able to speak without fear of reprisals, i.e. in "ideal speech situations" (ISS) (Habermas, 1984, 1987). ISS related to organisations could shed light on an exploration of older workers in modern society approached from a pragmatic perspective, to align to a systems structure and the everyday lifeworld of older workers to achieve an engaged, active, sustainable and fulfilled workforce.

References

AAT (Association of Accounting Technicians) (2015). *The Economic Benefits of Adults Reskilling*. London: Centre for Economics and Business Research Ltd (CEBR).

Altmann, R. (2014). *A New Vision for Older Workers: Retain, Retrain and Recruit*. London: Department for Work and Pensions.

Alvesson, M., and Wilmott, H. (Eds.). (1996). *Critical Management Studies*. London: Sage.

Armstrong-Stassen, M. (2008). 'Factors associated with job content plateauing among older workers'. *Career Development International, 13(7)*, 594–613.

Arvinen-Muondo, R., and Perkins, S. (Eds.). (2013). *Organizational Behaviour*. London: Kogan Page.

Barnett, R. (2012). *Imagining the University*. Abingdon, Oxon: Routledge.

Baumgartner, L. (2001). 'Four Adult Development Theories and Their Implications for Practice'. In *Focus on the Basics, Adult Development*, Vol. 5 (B), 29–34. National Center for the Study of Adult Learning and Literacy (NCSALL). www.ncsall.net/index.html@id=481.html [Accessed 24/1/2018].

Bingham, D., and Bubb, S. (2017). 'Leadership for Wellbeing'. In P. Earley and T. Greany (Eds.), *School Leadership and Education System Reform*. London: Bloomsbury.

Bingham, D.M. (2017). *Exploring Professional Development for Older Workers in the Higher Education Workplace* (Doctoral dissertation). UCL (University College London).

Bolman, L.G., and Deal, T.E. (2008). *Reframing Organizations: Artistry, Choice, and Leadership* (4th edn.). San Francisco, CA: Jossey-Bass.

Boxall, P., and Purcell, J. (2008). *Strategy and Human Resource Management* (2nd edn.). New York: Palgrave MacMillan.

Boxall, P., and Purcell, J. (2011). *Strategy and Human Resource Management* (3rd edn.). London: Palgrave Macmillan.

Brown, R., and Ohsako, T. (2003). 'A study of inter-generational programmes for schools promoting international education in developing countries through the International Baccalaureate Diploma Programme'. *Journal of Research in International Education, 2(2)*, 151–165.

Charytonowicz, J. (Ed.). (2014). 'Advances in human factors and sustainable infrastructure, advances in human factors and ergonomics', *5th International Conference on Applied Human Factors and Ergonomics*, 19–23 July 2014. Kraków, Poland.

CIPD (Chartered Institute of Personnel Development) (2011). *Managing Age*. London: CIPD.

Edge, K., Descours, K., and Oxley, L. (2017). 'Generation X leaders from London, New York and Toronto'. *Educational Management Administration & Leadership, 45(5)*, 863–883. doi:10.1177/1741143217717278.

Edwards, J. (1987). *Positive Discrimination, Social Justice and Social Policy*. London: Tavistock.

Elliott, C.J., and Turnbull, R.S. (2005). *Critical Thinking in Human Resource Development*. London and New York: Routledge.

The Equality Act (2010). www.legislation.gov.uk/ukpga/2010/15/section/149 [Accessed 15/6/2018].

Eurobarometer (2015). *Eurobarometer 437: Discrimination in the EU in 2015*. EU Open Data Portal. http://data.europa.eu/euodp/en/data/dataset/S2077_83_4_437_ENG [Accessed 8/8/2018].

European Commission (2013). *The Costs and Benefits of Diversity. A Study on Methods and Indicators A Study on Methods and Indicators to Measure the Cost-Effectiveness to Measure the Cost-Effectiveness of Diversity Policies in Enterprise*. Brussels: Centre for Strategy and Evaluation, European Commission.

European Commission European Employment Observatory Review (2012). *Employment Policies to Promote Active Ageing*. Luxembourg: Publications Office of the European Union.

Evans, K., Hodkinson, P., and Unwin, L. (Eds.). (2002). *Working to Learn: Transforming Learning in the Workplace*. Abingdon, Oxon: Routledge.

Findsen, B. (2015). 'Older workers' learning within organisations: issues and challenges'. *Educational Gerontology, 41(8)*, 582–589.

Findsen, B., and Formosa, M. (2011). *Lifelong Learning in Later Life: A Handbook on Older Adult Learning*. Rotterdam: Sense.

Gibson, J.J. (1979). *The Ecological Approach to Visual perception*. Boston: Houghton Lifflin.

Habermas, J. (1984). *The Theory of Communicative Action* (Vol. 1). Boston: Beacon Press.

Habermas, J. (1987). *The Theory of Communicative Action* (Vol. 2). Trans. T. McCarthy. Cambridge: Polity Press.

Hager, P. (2010). 'Theories of Workplace Learning'. In M. Malloch, L. Cairns, K. Evans and B. O'Connor (Eds.), *The Sage Handbook of Workplace Learning*. London: Sage.

Harteis, C., and Goller, M. (2014). 'New Skills for New Jobs: Work Agency as a Necessary Condition for Successful Lifelong Learning'. In T. Halttunen, M. Koivisto and S. Billett (Eds.), *Promoting, Assessing, Recognizing and Certifying Lifelong Learning – International Perspectives and Practices*. Dordrecht: Springer.

Hodkinson, P., Hodkinson, H., Evans, K., Kersh, N., Fuller, A., Unwin, L., and Senker, P. (2004). 'The significance of individual biography in workplace learning'. *Studies in the Education of Adults, 36(1)*, 6–25.

House of Commons (2018). *Older Workers and Employment Fourth Report of Session 2017–19, HC 359*. London: House of Commons. [Accessed 18/8/2018].

Huysman, M. (1999). 'Balancing Biases: A Critical Review of the Literature on Organizational Learning'. In M. Easterby-Smith, J. Burgoyne and L. Araujo (Eds.), *Organizational Learning and the Learning Organization*, 59–74. London: Sage.

Jarvis, P. (2001). *Learning in Later Life: An Introduction for Educators and Carers*. London: Kogan Page.

Jarvis, P. (2004). *Adult Education and Lifelong Learning: Theory and Practice*. Abingdon: Taylor and Francis.

Johnson, J., and Schwabenland, C. (2013). 'Managing Diverse Identities at Work'. In R. Arvinen-Muondo and S. Perkins (Eds.), *Organizational Behaviour: People, Process, Work and Human Resource Management*. London: Kogan Page.

Joyce, B., and Showers, B. (1980). 'Improving in-service training: the messages of research'. *Educational Leadership, 37(5)*, 379–385.

Kandola, R., and Fullerton, J. (2003). *Diversity in Action: Managing the Mosaic*. London: CIPD.

Kanfer, R., and Ackerman, P.L. (2004). 'Aging, adult development, and work motivation'. *Academy of Management Review, 29(3)*, 440–458.

Kirton, G., and Greene, A.M. (2005). *The Dynamics of Managing Diversity: A Critical Approach*. Oxford: Butterworth Heinemann.

Kooij, D., de Lange, A., Jansen, P., and Dikkers, J. (2008). 'Older workers' motivation to continue to work: five meanings of age: a conceptual review'. *Journal of Managerial Psychology, 23(4)*, 364–394.

Laitinen, I. (2015). Adult and Lifelong Learning as Tools for Organisational Adaptation and Change Management. *Journal of Adult and Continuing Education, 21(2)*.

McGann, M., Ong, R., Bowman, R., Duncan, A., Kimberley, H., and Biggs, S. (2016). *A Gendered Analysis of Age Discrimination among Older Jobseekers in Australia*. Bankwest Curtin Economics Centre Working Paper 16/01 Perth: Curtin University.

McNair, S. (2009). *Older People's Learning – An Action Plan*. Leicester: National Institute of Adult Continuing Education (England and Wales).

McNair, S. (2010). *A Sense of a Future – A Study of Training and Work in Later Life*. NIACE. http://shop.niace.org.uk/media/catalog/product/a/_/a_sense_of_a_future_short_report_final_web.pdf [Accessed 18/6/2018].

McNair, S. (2011). *Older People and Skills in a Changing Economy*. London: UK Commission for Employment and Skills.

OECD (2006). *The Work Longer, Live Longer Report*. Paris: The Organization for Economic Cooperation and Development (OECD).

OECD. (2013). *Skills Outlook 2013 – First Results from the Survey of Adult Skills*. The Organization for Economic Cooperation and Development (OECD). https://www.oecd-ilibrary.org/education/oecd-skills-outlook-2013_9789264204256-en. [Accessed on 24/10/2018].

Oosterwikj, R.E. (2015). *Policy Frameworks Concerning Older Workers – A Comparative Study of Policy Frameworks and Trade Union Involvement in Sweden and the Netherlands*. Institute of International Education, Stockholm University. Unpublished Thesis. http://su.diva-portal.org/smash/get/diva2:818650/FULLTEXT01.pdf [Accessed 24/8/2018].

Osborne, M. (2015). 'Editorial (pp1-2). In Laitinen. I. (2015). Adult and Lifelong Learning as tools for organisational adaptation and change management'. *Journal of Adult and Continuing Education, 21(2)*, 36–54.

Rhoades, A., and Shepherdson, N. (2011). *Built on Values: Creating an Enviable Culture that Outperforms the Competition*. San Francisco, CA: Jossey-Bass.

Ritzer, G. (2012). *Sociological Theory* (8th edn.). New York: McGraw Hill.

Sen, A. (1993). 'Capability and Well-being'. In M. Nussbaum and A. Sen (Eds.), *The Quality of Life*. Oxford: Clarendon Press.

Silverman, D. (2013). *Doing Qualitative Research-A Practical Handbook* (4th edn.). London: Sage.

Stoll, L., Bolam, R., McMahon, A., Wallace, M., and Thomas, S. (2006). 'Professional learning communities: a review of the literature'. *Journal of Educational Change, 7(4)*, 221–258.

Strauss, A.L., and Corbin, J. (1994). 'Grounded Theory Methodology'. In N.K. Denzin and Y.S. Lincoln (Eds.), *Handbook of Qualitative Research*. Thousand Oaks, CA: Sage.

Strauss, S. (2013). 'Implicit Bias and Employment Discrimination'. In M.A. Paludi (Ed.), *Women and Management*. CA: ABC Clio.

Syed, J., and Ozbilgin, M. (2009). 'A relational framework for international transfer of diversity management practices'. *International Journal of Human Resource Management, 13 (6)*, 873–897.

Terry, P.R. (1997). 'Habermas and education: knowledge, communication, discourse'. *Curriculum Studies, 5(3)*, 269–279.

Tikkanen, T., and Nyhan, B. (Eds.). (2006). *Promoting Lifelong Learning for Older Workers: An International Overview*. Cedefop Reference series 65. The European Centre for the Development of Vocational Training. Luxembourg: Office for Official Publications of the European Communities. www.cedefop.europa.eu/EN/publications/13019.aspx [Accessed 15/4/2018].

UNESCO (2015). *Re-Thinking Education*. Paris: UNESCO.

Unwin, L. (2009). *Connecting Workplace Learning and VET to Lifelong Learning, Beyond Current Horizons*. http://citeseerx.ist.psu.edu/viewdoc/download?doi=10.1.1.595.3271&rep=rep1&type=pdf [Accessed 18/6/2018].

Zachery, L. (2000). *The Mentor's Guide, Facilitating Effective Learning Relationship*. San Francisco, CA: Jossey-Bass.

8 Reflections and recommendations

This concluding chapter summarises key reflections, empirical findings and thought leadership making recommendations for future policy and practice for older workers and workplaces across a number of disciplinary areas. Older workers' learning is complex, multilayered and interdisciplinary theories help make sense of the field under study.

The central proposition of this book is that achieving human flourishing and potential is not the singular premise of younger workers; older workers have a legitimate claim to learning as *vessels of untapped potential*. How older workers might be drawn into the lifeworld of contemporary and future workplaces, challenging restrictions of modernity and alienation, through engagement in dialogue via ideal speech situations (ISS) (Habermas 1987), to achieve flourishing through enabling structures and processes has been presented.

This has led to a re-imagining of older workers' learning possibilities when their contribution is not always valued.

Two lenses are important in evaluating the role of older workplaces. Firstly, that of a social justice perspective in the right for all humans to develop their potential and flourish espoused by UNESCO (2015). Secondly, where organisations reflect a business case lens for an older workers' role where it either makes good business sense to reflect diversity to match and align with their customer base or where it is expedient in carrying out corporate social responsibility which reflects and aligns to their mission statement and values.

The assumptions in this book are based on the premise of the right to agency and empowerment in learning as an older worker where too often the default narrative is of decline. My theoretical lens is an advocacy, participatory and world view perspective. The literature emphasises the role of contextual factors, including social, cultural, organisational and other factors in workplace learning as being important for a study of older workers' learning and which have been underestimated. The inclusion of these factors along with other aspects, provide a platform to rethink the nature of continuing learning. It also represents a step forward to a theoretical grounding of how learning occurs for older workers transformed into praxis permitting a space to a shift of celebrating age.

The book has set out some responses to the changing nature and size of ageing workforces across countries, policy and organisational responses to address four interrelated areas of concern and challenges seen through the literature, empirical research and case studies which are:

a) participation of older people in the workforce, linked to the withdrawal from the job market
b) policies to increase employment
c) retention and underemployment of older workers
d) what development and training are in place and what further development opportunities and types will be needed to best offer older workers' flourishing.

Pulling together the reflections, it is helpful to look at the role of older workers through a frame of:

a) society and policy making
b) business/organisations/institutions
c) policymakers and governments
d) individuals.

Society and policy making

At a supranational level, the UN Sustainable Development Goals (SDGs) set out overarching aspirations for countries to work to inclusive and equitable, quality education and promotion of lifelong learning opportunities for all (UN 2015), while UNESCO (2015) emphasised that lifelong learning is central to achieving full employment and supporting equity and inclusion for all. The Work Longer, Live Longer Report (OECD 2006) called for an overhaul of employment/social policies, practices and attitudes to encourage work at an older age.

Solutions and adaptations

There is a role for intervention by regulation and government policy making to recognise a diversity of needs in the workplace as has been argued in this book and by a number of others (Tikkanen and Nyhan 2006; Altmann 2014).

An individual country's national policy and government regulation context, relative to age, strongly affects the participation of older workers in the labour market and their retirement decisions. For example, as seen in Chapter 1, two guidelines from the Agenda for New Skills and Jobs Initiative (EU 2011:9), to prolong working lives, are particularly relevant – work–life balance policies with the provision of affordable care and innovation in the way work is organised (Guideline 7) and developing a skilled workforce to respond to labour market needs and promoting lifelong learning efforts to focus on the employability of older workers (Guideline 8).

Some progress has been made across OECD countries (OECD 2015). Significantly though with countries adopting a faster rise in state pensions, programmes to support those remaining in employment through early interventions may not be in place soon enough, this may affect women disproportionately more than men due to retirement ages catching up with men.

The EAEA (2012) report on 34 countries indicated that impact has been made including an increase in employment of older workers and in the numbers choosing to work past retirement age. This same report highlighted several areas where the UK needed to improve its employment rate for older workers.

Google's purchase of Calico, a development company that researches and creates interventions that help people to live longer, healthier lives indicates that company's drive for leading on global, economic trends and innovations that impact not just the world of work, but the way we go about our lives. We can expect further companies to focus on not just health and well-being, but also how environmental factors like workspaces impact lifespans.

Businesses/organisations/institutions

As a future trend, organisations will struggle to balance societal culture and their corporate culture. The SRHM (2015) references two types of culture, that of societal culture which develops very slowly and becomes a part of a person's self-identity. Corporate culture comprises the values, beliefs and practices a company chooses to adopt. Organisations need to understand how to manage cultural distance – the gaps between cultures – and the points of friction. They also need to understand how and when to impose their corporate culture. As culture impacts productivity. Organisations are developing more of a sense of corporate responsibility as diversity moves centre stage. This is seen in some of the case studies in Chapter 5. But, as suggested, there may be a time gap while organisations wrestle with trying to achieve the most harmonious and productive workplaces.

A recognition of what diversity is in the workplace for older workers is slowly being discussed and developed. A company can help by taking that stigma away. Case studies and vignettes given in this book across different sectors and organisations around diversity management have informed understandings of diversity and inclusion, giving some examples of good practice to establish an enabling workforce culture for older workers and also for learning and development for the older workforce enacted by organisations.

In countries with ageing and aged populations, it is important to consider the motivation and dynamics of training and learning of the greying workforce (World Economic Forum 2017). There is a significant drop in the rates of participation in training activities in the 54-and-older age group relative to younger working cohorts. This dynamic seems to be driven by both declining employee perception regarding the benefits of training, as well as greater employer motivation to invest in training younger workers in whom they feel their investment may see a greater return over a longer period of time. Helping older workers understand the range of training opportunities available to them, and encouraging take-up, is vital.

Career counselling, mid-life career reviews and motivational campaigns can be particularly useful tools in helping older workers maintain and improve their skills and continue their professional development into the final stages of their careers.

Individuals

Transitions should be seen more as a theory of personal development within the life cycle where after a transition there is a time of disorientation which acts as a turning point for growth (Bridges and Bridges 2017) and self-renewal. This means that an older worker can view themselves in a permanent state of self-development which has no externally socially constructed cut-off point which can be a lever in reframing and re-imagining older workplaces and indeed in moving beyond one specific workplace, representing a form of dynamism in fast-changing, inherently unstable workplaces, as we will see more of in the future. This however, will need time for a reorientation of its own, as for far too long, there has been little value seen in transitions so that such a shift will need supporting with development and training.

Summary reflection

Spaces are required for engagement, with development approaches suited to older workers' needs and to combat vulnerability. Thus, Habermas's Theory of Communicative Action (1984, 1987) through ideal speech situations (ISS) for older workers is crucial.

The theory supports the realisation of the capability to flourish through having the right vectors in place, as Sen's (1993) capability approach suggests. The vector of dialogic spaces advanced by way of Habermas's Theory of Communicative Action (1984, 1987), through ideal speech situations (ISS), (which are communitarian rather than individual) acts as a mechanism for worker agency at the micro levels of the workplace, providing open and free spaces for dialogue for older workers to be agentic over what their learning and development needs are.

The implication of Habermas's theory is that it affords a voice for older workers, which then can lead to an empowered community of older workers, able to articulate from the bottom up what they value in development and what their developmental needs are, identify opportunities and engage in learning activities. It provides a theoretical basis for development for this group which transcends bureaucracy and a marketised environment.

Establishing Habermasian spaces for dialogue provide spaces where staff and management might come together to renegotiate and advance older worker contributions when they are not always valued supporting positive institution and department cultures to advance business goals.

Taking the theory of integration further, having an organisational practice of valuing older workers through critical diversity management would provide the foundation and culture for a more supportive environment to older workers through progressive organisational policy. This would support Sen's flourishing theories where all feel valued, talents utilised and organisational goals are met as advocated by Kirton and Greene (2005). Diversity management includes ensuring talents are well used and staff retained. Part of this is in creating a culture supportive to difference while discriminatory attitudes and beliefs are a factor in job market withdrawal suggested in an EU policy paper (EAEA 2012).

Social, cultural and organisational factors are relevant to older workers' workplace learning and learning as a process aligned with participation (Hager 2010). Learning appears embedded within workplace activity and affected by these factors, argued by Baumgartner (2001) and by Unwin (2009). Organisational policy for transitions is needed which recognises a blurring of personal, individual and workplace life as supported by Evans et al. (2002). Recognising there is vulnerability in transitions supports an equity and diversity approach to people management to build an inclusive workplace environment. This approach signals to older workers they are respected and valued through HR practices targeted at older employees and should benefit from respectful treatment from supervisors and peers which is stressed by Armstrong-Stassen (2008).

Multigenerational workplaces

Learning gaps could be overcome through knowledge (K), skills (S), abilities and attitudes (A), (Rhoades and Shepherdson 2011). But a valuing-all approach should include a broader holistic viewpoint envisaging a dialogue between organisation and employee recognising that competence development (knowledge, skills and attitude) is only one aspect in the process. Spaces for dialogue need strengthening to champion older workers. This should be built into staff training and discussion groups to break down preconceptions to show staff they are valued, implying a groundswell of similar, communitarian thinking or norms (Habermas 1984:85–101, 284–288) and important for organisational culture as older workers who reported feeling more valued were more likely to talk about positive workplace interactions and relations with younger workers as noted by Ng and Law (2014).

Union advocacy, where possible, should be strengthened to play a more visible role through their equality units representing Habermas's reconceptualisation (1971). Older workers, in exercising work agency, should be more proactive contributors to consultative committees to self-initiate their development and in meetings with unions. Dialogical spaces should be established for more formalised intergenerational learning and peer-to-peer learning as argued by Findsen and Formosa (2011), resulting in innovation of benefit to organisations and staff, where stereotyping can be challenged for more harmonious and productive workplaces as Zachery (2000) suggests.

McNair (2010) anticipates creating a *sense of a positive future* as a major influence on work and training decisions, supporting an argument for older workers not just as a business case but a social justice one which could be mutually beneficial, and viewed as supportive by Armstrong-Stassen (2008). This approach recognises the urgency to reflect on professional development approaches and goals in the second half of life to protect against both unemployment and remain employable (McNair 2006; Altmann 2014). It results in a changing perspective where development moves from a maintenance perspective to a development perspective and where *mainstreaming progression becomes the norm*. The revised conceptual framework which has framed the recommendations which follow shifts older workers from being a burden to vessels of untapped potential, aligned to Habermas's reconceptualisation of a rationalised organisation (1990). Adler et al. (2007) suggested the shift considers the distribution of life chances of individuals through making more than minor adjustments, with older workers staking a rightful claim in the workplace, reenvisioning learning spaces for older workers and career progression.

Staff participants in the HE study suggested an inclusive workplace environment to support transitions through a valuing all approach which included:

- Recognition of caring responsibilities;
- Having voice for transitions (fora, discussions);
- Equitable access to development lost through caring responsibilities;
- Older workers' health issues;
- Developing self-esteem and work agency for empowerment.

Recommendations

Recommendations arising from the HE study, and further wider research findings relate to organisation diversity management, dialogue to challenge culture and unconscious bias for mutual benefit, empowerment and confidence in changing demographics and professional development approaches. They also relate to line management development, organisational learning policy, positive workplace climates to reverse plateauing, mobility and career progression being viewed as implicit, understanding and recognition of the positive benefits of both knowledge sharing, intergenerational, intragenerational sharing and promoting of careers through greater investment in training.

Organisational diversity management

A business case for diversity recognises changing demographics at the meso and micro-organisational level by no longer ignoring talent from wherever it comes. Strategic plans, HR documentation, equality policies and staff development plans may in places need redrafting to reference age, drawing on wider policy and making reference to equality data reports. Bolman and Deal suggest a case for diversity (2008) based on a diverse society, although these authors stop short of advocating for the explicit benefits of a diverse workforce which Boxall and Purcell (2011) and Green (2010) have proposed.

In the UK, the DWP (DWP 2013) have argued that innovative practices eradicating unfair or discriminatory treatment make sound business sense and are an effective means of signalling and maintaining a reputation as a highly respected employer and a champion of equality. There is a need for a critical HRD approach and critical HRD cannot ignore trade union involvement any longer, which has a large role to play. Awareness raising campaigns could be implemented on the basis that we are all going to get old.

Recommendations include:

- Conducting an organisational readiness audit. For example, the NHS Working Longer Group (2017) has produced a checklist for the ageing workforce
- Implementation of an annual staff survey to track progress in developing the organisation as a workplace based on diversity management
- Involving unions which are undertaking audits and surveys into age diversity
- Conducting longer term research considering what is progressive organisational policy making in relation to age (Syed and Ozbilgin 2009)
- Adoption of age positive logos.

Dialogue – challenging culture and unconscious bias for mutual benefit

Fora, working groups and other ways of showing older staff they are valued could support this group. These findings explicitly link to Habermas's theories of communitarianism (1984, 1987). Furthermore, instituting intergenerational meetings can develop positive institution and department cultures advancing business goals which are positive for staff and management, as suggested by Findsen's work (2015).

Paying attention to, and formalising ways of working, is one method to extend participation and to challenge entrenched cultural ideas through reaching across generations.

- Consistent team building staff development across different and the same departments facilitated by an expert.

Careful attention should be paid to creating a culture supportive of difference thereby challenging unconscious assumptions and bias as suggested by Strauss (2013). The adoption of age-neutral language should be encouraged aligned to the Altmann report (2014). Some strategies to reduce unconscious bias but not necessarily only related to age as identified by Traub (2014) include:

> - Becoming more aware of our biases and purposively strive to change them
> - Conducting an audit of the workplace by critical assessment of interview, hiring, promotion and termination practice
> - Administer organisation-wide surveys to specifically assess stereotypes and biases
> - Customised training and development for hidden bias, stereotypical behaviours and forms of unfairness
> - Establish team members of diverse groups
> - Create projects and images that portray older workers in a positive light to diminish stereotyping
> - Creation of an environment in which it is safe to disagree and discuss various viewpoints
> - Creation of an ombudsperson role and responsibility who is knowledgeable about unconscious bias.
>
> (Traub 2014:4)

Empowerment and confidence in changing demographics

Empowerment is critical in the development of work agency. A strong focus on empowerment and confidence though staff development and within departments is needed, perhaps supported by a buddy system.

- Skills assessment and needs analysis identifying achievements and gaps to support confidence, acting as a bridge to future progression;
- Creation of spaces for individual or departmental dialogue, discussion groups/fora, decision-making tools and the use of facilitators representing role models;
- Ensure portrayal of older workers in various organisational media e.g. websites, annual reports.

Learning and development approaches

The OECD (2006) agenda for reform for older workers views employers as gatekeepers with one approach being that of greater investment in older workers training, as there is better ROI through longer pay-off time, as well as offering wider benefits to society and individuals.

A PwC report "Workforce of the Future" (2018) considers that adaptability will be a key future ingredient in successful organisations and that it is not just organisations that must adapt but individuals and society.

As discussed in this book, it is not possible to predict the precise skills that will be needed even five years from now (PwC 2018) but having a readiness for change is a skill that individuals and organisations will need to learn and hone. This will mean a readiness to shoulder the responsibility for your own learning in acquiring skills and experience over a lifetime, a readiness to have the confidence to try out new skills and experiences where the concept of having work agency will be crucial, particularly for older workers who are often held back by negative views of themselves and stereotyping by society. It requires a readiness, and robustness to adopt a life time of learning mental approach and the preparedness to be ready to retrain and rethink a career.

It will be helpful to think about a career as an ongoing series of career cycles, where you might expect to plateau out in a job and see that as a motivation to leap forward and address a new career. This requires creativity and self-motivation as an individual. Sometimes as Gratton and Scott (2016) indicate it is not a question of always climbing the ladder but thinking about a lateral move as you look to exploit the skills that you have gained on your career journey. Within this, transitions would need to be built into the cycles, with support and help given.

Younger generations are becoming used to this way of working, now it is for older individuals to replenish their careers. There should, and must be, an accent on supporting people in the development and sustained sparking of creativity and innovation which is inherent in humans. This is where the re-imagining of the workplaces comes in for older workers, where increasingly problem-solving and cognitive skills will be needed. There is no space for plateauing.

However, individuals should not be on their own, it is also down to organisations and government policymakers to provide enabling levers. The support from organisations should take the form of a change management structure that enables and empowers older workers to consistently flourish and have mobility within an organisation and the support to move on out of that organisation. As the PwC report indicates, both government policymakers and organisations have a role in the supply side through pathways to training and retraining (2018). Trade unions too have a large role to play in championing training and development and in protecting older workers' rights.

Regardless of our inability to predict the exact skills that will be required even in the near future, development for older workers should take a form that recognises progress and the enhancement of older workers' roles so as to support motivation and engagement. This could take the form of:

- A personal professional development plan that would be motivational and individual, representing ownership;

- Age specific provision is necessary, aligned to equality and diversity for older workers' best interests;
- Refresh skills and reengage older workers with different types development to reengage with the exterior, e.g. increased IT and digital training.

An organisation could gain competitive advantage by recognising the role of informal learning through the following measures:

- A funded coaching service cascaded down;
- Confidence booster training and discussion groups;
- Reangling the professional development portfolio to capture and evaluate self-reflective learning where informal learning can be formalised alongside formal learning (TLRP 2000–09);
- Implementing leadership skills for all with a view to everyone having the capability to lead and not just the preserve for the few.

Future career progression development might be facilitated by the following steps:

- Establishing annual reviews as a performance management and development tool;
- Longer term planning, at least a 12-month plan with access to a coach or career service as the norm;
- Establishment of personal professional development plans as a component part of the annual review, reviewed at intervals and shared with a coach/buddy;
- HR work undertaken at strategic level to offer clear career pathways and policies.

The US based Society for Human Resource Management (SRHM) (2015) suggests that effective development programmes for older workers should offer the following:

- A clear definition of what the organisation wants to achieve;
- Identification of target groups that are most critical to achieving organisational goals;
- A development plan for target groups;
- Integration of effective adult-learning principles into the design of the development programme;
- Assessment of the success of the development programme against organisational goals.

Turning to digital literacy, it has been suggested that capability to use computers and information technology can affect motivation and ability for self-learning (Wang 2018).

And that a lack of computer skills can affect older people's sense of security. Therefore, this type of development should be addressed with care so that confidence is not lost. Digital literacies are defined as being/having the capabilities which fit someone for living, learning, working, participating and thriving in a digital society. To become digitally literate means developing function skills, attitudes, values and behaviours that can be categorised under:

- Digital identity, wellbeing, safety and security;
- Communication, collaboration and participation;
- Teaching, learning and personal/professional development;
- Technical proficiency;
- Information, data and media literacies;
- Creation, innovation and scholarship.

However, a further suggestion is that rather than proposing a simple competency framework digital literacies that bring real benefit to users/learners in terms of confidence, competence and capabilities and, most importantly, well-being will be developmental and supportive tools that empowers and enables extending digital capabilities to be able to live, learn, work, participate and thrive in our complex, ever-changing digital world.

(Kennedy, S. n.d. Health Education England).

The role of government and policy making in developing true learning opportunities for digital workplace readiness

In line with Sen's notions of flourishing, the World Economic Forum recognises that it is a human right to flourish through learning (WEF 2017). Therefore, respective governments must provide the necessary support and empower individual learners as its "An Agenda for Leaders to Shape the Future of Education, Gender and Work White Paper" report (2017) recommends. This is necessary for global readiness for digital workplaces and to ensure the potential of all human capital is realised. But to achieve human potential for development, there must be acknowledgement in an organisation's policies and practices and in government legislation that sufficient time and opportunity is awarded for true and sustainable development and learning and not merely play lip service to it.

Line management training

Line managers need to adopt specific approaches, understanding how age impacts perception, feelings and confidence. Line managers should be given the necessary tools to support individuals and assist them in exploring other opportunities as recommended by Altmann (2014).

Organisational policy climate for learning

A learning organisation should be implemented in every organisation, which includes Illeris (2004) competence development and considers praxis of action of educational gerontology (Findsen and Formosa 2011). Informal learning away from the workplace should be recognised, at least as significant as formal learning, and should be valued and used as part of the formal process in reviews of development undertaken (TLRP 2000–09).

Expectations and empowerment for development and reversing plateauing

An organisational model would include a positive workplace climate for empowerment and the development of work agency. Placing responsibility to develop firmly in both the worker and organisation's expectations makes up the expectation part of the learning landscape. This helps with engagement as workers transition and where an employee will feel disposed to the organisation, retaining the psychological contract. There should be an opportunity and clear anticipation of rethinking skills, how older workers use them and how they might improve them (McNair 2011; Altmann 2014).

Mobility and career progression

Offering development for self-employment helps organisational movement and succession planning in a pyramidal structure and is mutually beneficial (OECD 2011) with a career service offered in tandem. As a Deloitte report (2017) makes clear, learning should encourage and even push people to move across jobs to increase mobility referring to adaptation of HR policies that support people to adapt to opening up to mobility, in what is termed intelligent assistance. However, such a strategy comes with a caution as self-motivation is individual, and a forcing policy will most likely not result in increased productivity or performance and at worst could result in an early exit from the workplace.

Knowledge sharing

There is evidence of gaining value from and giving value to others in knowledge sharing. Knowledge sharing helps break down silos and encourages more effective working. Utilising skills and knowledge in different ways can bestow continued value on workers moving to the last five or ten years of a working career as Findsen and Formosa (2011) suggested.

Intergenerational and intragenerational sharing and team working

The value of mixed age workplace communities should be recognised (Findsen and Formosa 2011). There should also be an acknowledgement that healthy communities have a mixture of age groups, while business effectiveness is improved through team working of those age groups (Barnett 2012).

Dewey's understanding of education as a process of supplying the conditions which insure growth, or adequacy of life, irrespective of age (1995:100) implies the need to offer opportunities for young people to cooperate with older people to help them make sense of the world. Intergenerational learning can be seen as a process through which individuals of all ages acquire skills and knowledge, as well as attitudes and values, from daily experience, all available resources, and the influences in their own "life worlds" (FIM NewLearning 2008). However, it should also be understood that sharing of knowledge across generations can be difficult in hierarchical structures. This coincides with a call for increased interdisciplinary skills development recognising an organisational shift to networks of teams (Deloitte 2017) and a loosening of vertical structures.

Improving wellbeing for older workers

This book has emphasised the necessity of holistic responses for older workers' working conditions and well-being. Aligned to this, the Taylor Review (2017) makes the point that the shape and content of work and individual health and well-being are strongly related. For the benefit for firms, workers and the public interest much more needs to be done around workplace health and well-being in ageing workplaces (Bingham and Bubb 2017).

> With more and more people working well into their sixties, many individuals will now spend around 50 years of their life in paid work. As such, work is strongly related to the quality of individuals' lives and their well-being. Quality jobs increase participation rates, productivity and economic performance, whereas, low-quality work can push people out of the labour market or in to work which does not fully utilise their skills and experience, reducing well-being and productivity.
>
> (Taylor Review 2017:98)

Recommendations from the UK's National Institute for Health and Clinical Excellence (NICE) guidance in 2015 on organisational commitment to make health and well-being a core priority for top management in the NHS, the UK's national health service and the largest employer in Europe, will be relevant to other sectors and situations. The guidance places a clear emphasis on the strategic importance and benefits of healthy workplaces, encouraging a consistent, positive approach for all. The guidance is clear that top managers with remit for workplace health should address the issues of:

- physical work environment;
- mental wellbeing at work;
- fairness, justice, participation, and trust;
- senior leadership;
- line managers' role, leadership style, and training;
- job design.

Workplace health is also reflected in the ability to work flexibly. PriceWaterhouseCoopers (PwC) the global accounting firm, have in 2018, announced a flexible scheme that will allow new joiners to ostensibly work when they want, and as many hours as they want in a jettisoning of the full-time contract and standard working hours.

This is in the acknowledgement of the gig economy, that some workers are wanting to forgo traditional working patterns and are more motivated by the opportunity to work flexibly and a satisfactory work–life balance than remuneration. People will be able to choose shorter hours or only working for a few months a year. PwC are also offering a restart to careers through a six-month paid senior internship programme "Back to Business" designed to support senior professionals restart their career after an extended break.

Closing comments

Stereotypical definitions of ageing and retirement are no longer relevant both in terms of a traditional view of age and the activities that are associated with it. Moreover, negative stereotypes and discrimination positively hinder economic development as increasing numbers of older workers are required to fill unfilled jobs as the demographic gap widens.

It is clear from research that later age workers workers want to contribute, and employers need their knowledge, experience and the expertise that they bring. Older workers are to be valued as an important business and societal asset to be recruited, retained and developed creating workplaces of mutual benefit.

Human resource management has been identified as one of the key factors in remaining in work. Work motivation may be improved by organisational strategies and managerial practices taking account normative patterns of adult development (Kanfer and Ackerman 2004). Most significantly declining health and career plateaus should and can be countered through human resource management policies and practices including ergonomic adjustments and continuous career development (Kooij et al. 2008).

Motivation has been identified in the literature as one of the key factors contributing to remaining at work until older age. While it is becoming clearer, some of the motivators for those over 50+ to remain at work until an older age require further research and there is sparse theoretical understanding on the differing aspects of motivation in relation to learning, for example, in how collaboration is conducted in learning and coconstruction of knowledge for this older group, and in the actual practise of how knowledge utilisation and supporting others to gain knowledge operates. Also, a clearer understanding of the effects of ageing and adult development on work motivation and how best to motivate and manage older workers is required. These aspects need further investigation (Eurofound 2017) as more traditional views of work motivation to do not appear to apply.

The 2018 annual World Economic Forum in Davos, discussing global research conducted in 12 countries, with 7,000 adults and 600 senior leaders from private and government sectors identifies critical imperatives for financial security in the areas of health, action, technology and structures. Crucially, it is suggested that ageing workforces may be the next global concern when 70% of millennials expect to keep working later in life to maintain their desired quality of life and where two out of three adults expect to live past 80, but where only one in three anticipate having enough money to afford it.

The World Economic Forum's Expert Network and the Global Coalition on Aging state:

> There is also an opportunity to better leverage the abilities of those over 60, by adjusting workplace policies and redefining what "retirement" means. Investing more significantly in healthier ageing processes can help combat related health conditions, improve functional ability, and increase productivity. A transformation of institutional structures is called for, alongside public policies better aligned to the world's new demographic makeup.
>
> World Economic Forum (n.d.)

This book has contributed to a holistic and more nuanced understanding of multiple facets of older workers' learning having generated new perspectives on the value placed on development for older workers. It has explored what forms are valuable and why, exploring similarities and differences and gaps for learning seen between older workers and management. It has shed light on types of learning and development to understand how these forms of learning are informed gaining insights into vocabulary, practices and approaches for development. Finally, strategic recommendations at the meso- and micro-organisational level have been made.

It is critical for older workers, both societally and economically, to have opportunities for development, capability and enabling workplace structures. The area of transitions in the workplace linked to adult learning perspectives is underresearched. More widely, the area of educational gerontology is still evolving and is still to find its place as a subset of adult and lifelong learning. It is hoped that this book goes some way towards the ambition of seeing older people as having the potential for continued growth and having their learning needs in the workplace addressed.

Developing older workers creates opportunities for progression for mutual benefit when organisations succeeding in the global information society are those that can identify, value, create and evolve their knowledge assets. Also, where high levels of work-related skills and occupational knowledge can secure long-term employment and employability (OECD 2012), promotion and work-related progression (Goller and Billett 2014). However, we need to be very mindful of what Biesta calls the "politics of learning" where lifelong learning is only seen for purposes of the economy and that it is still up to us as individuals to make decisions around whether we learn or not (Biesta 2018:256).

Older workers doubtless pose challenges for organisations which includes providing healthcare and occupational health for a grouping that will experience four-and-a-half times as many disabilities as younger groupings

(Tishman et al. 2012) and where adaptations will be required in the form of flexible working and a move from physically demanding work.

However, with advances in technology and automation the latter will be alleviated and reduced, where physical types of jobs will be changed or augmented. The US SRHM report (Hitch and Kirkman 2013) makes clear that in increasingly global workforces this will mean combining differing management and work styles based on individual cultures which can vary hugely in terms of attitudes to power. The opportunity and the challenges will be in matching across the right job roles, incentives and retraining opportunities for each worker, avoiding age discrimination practices.

As societies age, we are reminded that there are positive physical and psychological effects to working longer which can lead to happier and more productive lives through maintaining identity and a sense of purpose; social interaction and connectivity; the value and rewards of having paid employment in:

- Maintaining identity and sense of purpose;
- Sustaining productive engagement;
- Physically demanding jobs and their contribution to physical health for those 65 and over;
- Social interaction and connectivity;
- Value of job related rewards.

Source: Tishman et al. (2018)

Taking the idea of learning a step further, we are also reminded that working is both an economic and societal concept. Given the importance of cities to society, growing numbers of regions, cities and communities are adopting initiatives through the UNESCO Global Network of Learning Cities (GNLC), allowing citizens of all ages to refresh, work on their skills and competencies throughout their lives in a lifelong learning environment as learning cities, the idea being to adopt a lifelong learning philosophy (UNESCO 2013).

As such a philosophy takes further root we should anticipate a positive future for older workers and a groundswell of communitarian thinking and norms as Habermas (1984) sees it through the expansion of new learning and working spaces where the expectation to flourish in a working life-world that supports older workers for an engaged and fulfilled workforce becomes the norm.

References

Adler, P.S., Forbes, L.C., and Willmott, H. (2007). '3 critical management studies'. *The Academy of Management Annals, 1(1)*, 119–179. doi:10.1080/078559808.

Altmann, R. (2014). *A New Vision for Older Workers: Retain, Retrain and Recruit.* London: Department for Work and Pensions.

Armstrong-Stassen, M. (2008). 'Factors associated with job content plateauing among older workers'. *Career Development International, 13(7)*, 594–613.

Barnett, R. (2012). *Imagining the University*. Abingdon, Oxon: Routledge.

Baumgartner, L. (2001). 'Four Adult Development Theories and Their Implications for Practice'. In *Focus on the Basics, Adult Development*, Vol. 5 (B), 29–34. National Center for the Study of Adult Learning and Literacy (NCSALL). www.ncsall.net/index.html@id=481.html [Accessed 24/1/2018].

Biesta, G. (2018). 'Interrupting the Politics of Learning'. In K. Illeris (Ed.), *Contemporary Theories of Learning* (2nd edn.). London: Routledge.

Bingham, D., and Bubb, S. (2017). 'Leadership for Wellbeing'. In P. Earley and T. Greany (Eds.), *School Leadership and Education System Reform*. London: Bloomsbury.

Bolman, L.G., and Deal, T.E. (2008). *Reframing Organizations: Artistry, Choice, and Leadership* (4th edn.). San Francisco, CA: Jossey-Bass.

Boxall, P., and Purcell, J. (2011). *Strategy and Human Resource Management* (3rd edn.). London: Palgrave Macmillan.

Bridges, W., and Bridges, S. (2017). *Managing Transitions: Making the Most of Change* (Revised 4th edn.). London: Nicholas Brealey.

Deloitte (2017). *The Global Human Capital Trends 2017*. Deloitte University Press. https://www2.deloitte.com/insights/us/en/focus/human-capital-trends/2017.html.

Department for Work and Pensions (DWP) (2013). *Management of an Ageing Workforce*. www.gov.uk/government/publications/management-of-an-ageing-workforce/management-of-an-ageing-workforce [Accessed 6/9/2018].

Dewey, J. (1995). 'Education as Growth'. In R.B. Goodman (Ed.), *Pragmatism: A Contemporary Reader*, 93–103. London: Routledge.

European Association for Education of Adults (EAEA) (2012). *Older Learning – Learning Later in Life*. Policy Paper. www.eaea.org/media/policy-advocacy/eaea-statements/2012_eaea_policy-paper_active-ageing.pdf.

EU (2011). *Agenda for New Skills and Jobs Initiative*. Luxembourg: Publications Office of the European Union.

Eurofound (2017). *Working Conditions of Workers of Different Ages: European Working Conditions Survey 2015*. Luxembourg: Publications Office of the European Union.

Evans, K., Hodkinson, P., and Unwin, L. (Eds.). (2002). *Working to Learn: Transforming Learning in the Workplace*. Abingdon, Oxon: Routledge.

FIM-NewLearning (2008). *Intergenerational Learning in Europe: Policies, Programmes & Practical Guidance*. www.menon.org/wp-content/uploads/2012/11/final-report.pdf.

Findsen, B. (2015). 'Older workers' learning within organisations: issues and challenges'. *Educational Gerontology, 41(8)*, 582–589.

Findsen, B., and Formosa, M. (2011). *Lifelong Learning in Later Life: A Handbook on Older Adult Learning*. Rotterdam: Sense.

Goller, M., and Billett, S. (2014). 'Agentic Behaviour at Work: Crafting Learning Experiences'. In C. Harteis, A. Rausch and J. Seifried (Eds.), *Discourses on Professional Learning*, 25–44. Netherlands: Springer.

Gratton, L., and Scott, A. (2016). *The 100 Year Life*. London: Bloomsbury.

Green, D. (2010). *Reframing Organizations Artistry, Choice, and Leadership, Lee G. Bolman and Terrence E. Deal*. [PowerPoint Presentation] www.drdouggreen.com/wp-content/Reframing-Organizations.pdf.

Habermas, J. (1971). *Knowledge and Human Interests*. Trans. J.J. Shapiro. London: Polity Press.

Habermas, J. (1984). *The Theory of Communicative Action*. Vol. I. Boston: Beacon Press.

Habermas, J. (1987). *The Theory of Communicative Action*. Vol. 2. Trans. T. McCarthy. Cambridge: Polity Press.

Habermas, J. (1990). *Moral Consciousness and Communicative Action*. Cambridge: Polity Press.

Hager, P. (2010). 'Theories of Workplace Learning'. In M. Malloch, L. Cairns, K. Evans and B. O'Connor (Eds.), *The Sage Handbook of Workplace Learning*. London: Sage.

Hitch, C., and Kirkman, B. (2013). *Engaging Older workers Strategically*. Virginia: Society for Human Resource Management (SRHM) Foundation.

Illeris, K. (2004). 'A model for learning in working life'. *Journal of Workplace Learning, 16 (8)*, 431–441. doi:10.1108/13665620410566405/.

Kanfer, R., and Ackerman, P.L. (2004). 'Aging, adult development, and work motivation'. *Academy of Management Review, 29(3)*, 440–458.

Kennedy, S. (n.d.). *Health Education England and Building a Digital Ready Workforce*. https://digileaders.com/digital-literacy-nhs/.

Kirton, G., and Greene, A.M. (2005). *The Dynamics of Managing Diversity: A Critical Approach*. Oxford: Butterworth Heinemann.

Kooij, D., de Lange, A., Jansen, P., and Dikkers, J. (2008). 'Older workers' motivation to continue to work: five meanings of age: a conceptual review'. *Journal of Managerial Psychology, 23(4)*, 364–394.

McNair, S. (2006). *Older People's Learning: An Action Plan*. NIACE: Leicester.

McNair, S. (2010). *A Sense of a Future – A Study of Training and Work in Later Life*. NIACE. http://shop.niace.org.uk/media/catalog/product/a/_/a_sense_of_a_future_short_report_final_web.pdf [Accessed 18/6/2018].

McNair, S. (2011). *Older People and Skills in a Changing Economy*. London, UK: Commission for Employment and Skills.

National Institute for Health and Clinical Excellence (NICE) (2015). *Workplace Health: Management Practices NICE Guideline [NG13]*. [updated March 2016] www.nice.org.uk/guidance/ng13/chapter/Recommendations [Accessed 2/8/2018].

Ng, E.S.W., and Law, A. (2014). 'Keeping up! older workers' adaptation in the workplace after age 55'. *Canadian Journal on Aging, 33(1)*, 1–14.

NHS Working Longer Group (2017) *Supporting Your Staff*. www.nhsemployers.org/your-workforce/need-to-know/working-longer-group/working-longer-group-tools-and-resources/the-ageing-workforce-a-resource-for-managers/thinking-about-and-supporting-your-team [Accessed 1/9/2018].

OECD (2006). *The Work Longer, Live Longer Report*. Paris: The Organization for Economic Cooperation and Development (OECD).

OECD (2011). *Pensions at a Glance 2011: Retirement-Income Systems in OECD and G20 Countries*. OECD. http://dx.doi.org/10.1787/pension_glance-2011-en.

OECD (2012). *OECD Employment Outlook*. Paris: The Organization for Economic Cooperation and Development (OECD).

OECD (2015). *Education at a Glance 2015*. Paris: OECD.

PriceWaterhouseCoopers (PwC) (2018). *Workforce of the Future – The Competing Forces Shaping 2030*. www.pwc.com/people [Accessed 20/8/2018].

Rhoades, A., and Shepherdson, N. (2011). *Built on Values: Creating an Enviable Culture that Outperforms the Competition*. San Francisco, CA: Jossey-Bass.

Sen, A. (1993). 'Capability and Well-being'. In M. Nussbaum and A. Sen (Eds.), *The Quality of Life*. Oxford: Clarendon Press.

Society for Human Resource Management (SRHM) (2015). *Future Global Trends Affecting Your Organization – Engaging and Integrating a Global Workforce*. Society for Human Resource Management (SRHM) Foundation. http://futurehrtrends.eiu.com/report-2014/executive-summary/ [Accessed 18/7/2018].

Strauss, S. (2013). 'Implicit Bias and Employment Discrimination'. In M.A. Paludi (Ed.), *Women and Management*. CA: ABC Clio.

Syed, J., and Ozbilgin, M. (2009). 'A relational framework for international transfer of diversity management practices'. *International Journal of Human Resource Management, 13(6)*, 873–897.

Taylor, M. (2017). *Good Work: The Taylor Review of Modern Working Practices*. Tech. rep. London: Department for Business, Energy and Industrial Strategy.

Tikkanen, T., and Nyhan, B. (Eds.). (2006). *Promoting Lifelong Learning for Older Workers: An International Overview*. Cedefop Reference series 65. The European Centre for the Development of Vocational Training. Luxembourg: Office for Official Publications of the European Communities. www.voced.edu.au/content/ngv%3A25170 [Accessed 6/9/2018].

Tishman, F., Van Looy, S., and Bruyère, S. (2012). *Employer Strategies for Responding to an aging Workforce*. NTAR Leadership Center. Boston: Center for Retirement Research at Boston College.

Tishman, F., Van Looy, S., and Bruyère, S. (2018). *Employer Strategies for Responding to an Aging Workforce*. www.researchgate.net/publication/266870464_Employer_Strategies_for_Responding_to_an_Aging_Workforce_Employer_Strategies_for_Responding_to_an_Aging_Workforce [Accessed 1/9/2018].

TLRP (Teaching and Learning Research Programme) (2000–09). ESRC. www.tlrp.org/index.html. [Accessed 2/9/2018].

Traub, L. (2014). *Ten Strategies to Support Your Unconscious Bias Initiative's ROI*. Cook Ross Inc. http://cookross.com/free-thought-papers/ [Accessed 18/8/2018].

UN Sustainable Development Goals (2015). *Transforming Our World: The 2030 Agenda for Sustainable Development*. https://sustainabledevelopment.un.org/post2015/transformingourworld [Accessed 15/8/2018].

UNESCO (2013). *Education Transforms Lives*. Paris: UNESCO. http://uil.unesco.org/lifelong-learning/learning-cities [Accessed 15/9/2018].

UNESCO (2015). *Re-thinking Education*. Paris: UNESCO.

Unwin, L. (2009). *Connecting Workplace Learning and VET to Lifelong Learning*. Beyond Current Horizons. http://citeseerx.ist.psu.edu/viewdoc/download?doi=10.1.1.595.3271&rep=rep1&type=pdf [Accessed 18/6/2018].

Wang, R. (2018). 'Conference presentation. 56th session of the UN's commission for social development'. Strategies for Eradicating Poverty to Achieve Sustainable Development for All. United Nations Headquarters: New York, 29 January to 7 February 2018. http://agewell-nce.ca/archives/6333 [Accessed 5/9/2018].

World Economic Forum (2017). *An Agenda for Leaders to Shape the Future of Education, Gender and Work White Paper'* Report (2017), World Economic Forum.

World Economic Forum (n.d.). *Expert Network and the Global Coalition on Aging*. https://toplink.weforum.org/knowledge/insight/a1Gb0000000LHRxEAO/explore/summary [Accessed 19/7/2018].

Zachery, L. (2000). *The Mentor's Guide Facilitating Effective Learning Relationship*. San Francisco, CA: Jossey-Bass.

Index

For Product Safety Concerns and Information please contact our EU representative GPSR@taylorandfrancis.com Taylor & Francis Verlag GmbH, Kaufingerstraße 24, 80331 München, Germany